BOLIVIA
in Pictures

Francesca Davis DiPiazza

Twenty-First Century Books

Contents

Twenty-First Century Books
A division of Lerner Publishing Group, Inc.
241 First Avenue North
Minneapolis, MN 55401 U.S.A.

Website address: www.lernerbooks.com

web enhanced @ www.vgsbooks.com

CULTURAL LIFE 46

► Religion. Fiestas, Holidays, and Sports.
Literature. Language. Art. Music. Clothing. Food.

THE ECONOMY 58

► Services and Tourism. Transportation and
Communications. Industry and Oil and Natural Gas.
Mining. Manufacturing. Agriculture. Livestock,
Fishing, and Forestry. Illegal Drug Trade. The Future.

FOR MORE INFORMATION

Library of Congress Cataloging-in-Publication Data

DiPiazza, Francesca, 1961–
    Bolivia in pictures / by Francesca Davis DiPiazza.
        p. cm. — (Visual geography series)
    Includes bibliographical references and index.
    ISBN 978-0-8225-8568-8 (lib. bdg. : alk. paper)
    1. Bolivia—Juvenile literature. I. Title.
F3308.5.D57 2008
984.0022'2—dc22   2007022061

Manufactured in the United States of America
1 2 3 4 5 6 – BP – 13 12 11 10 09 08

INTRODUCTION

The nation of Bolivia is sometimes called the rooftop of South America. Half of the nation's 9.2 million people live in the Andes Mountains. La Paz, Bolivia, is the world's highest capital city, at a height of 12,000 feet (3,658 meters) above sea level. The only other place in the world where people live this high is Tibet, in central Asia.

Bolivia is a land of contrasts. From snowy, barren Andes peaks in the west, the land descends to windy plains and steep tropical valleys. Farther east, vast grassy plains become swamps in the wet season. Rivers thread through dense Amazon rain forests in the northeast, while the rough southeast experiences near-desert conditions.

About 500 B.C., Aymara-speaking peoples in the Bolivian Andes established the Tiwanakan civilization. Sophisticated artists and engineers built roads, temples, and water systems. But the Tiwanakans did not leave written records. The civilization disappeared about A.D. 1200, possibly because of drought. Two hundred years later, their lands became part of the Inca Empire. The Incas unified many different

groups, in part by making them all use the Quechua language. The language, along with Aymara, is one of modern Bolivia's official languages. Spanish conquerors defeated the Inca Empire in 1532 and took over its lands.

The Spanish ruled the region of present-day Bolivia, which they called Upper Peru. Spanish colonists seized land and exploited the people. Meanwhile, Spain grew wealthy from Upper Peru's huge silver deposits. The independent nation of Bolivia was not born until 1825, after the fifteen-year War of Independence. The country took its name from the South American liberator Simón Bolívar.

Many short-lived governments came and went in the years after Bolivia's independence. Members of the military often seized control of the government. At independence, Bolivia was a very large country whose land included a strip along the Pacific coast. But the country fought with its neighbors, and it lost all the wars it fought. Bolivia was forced to give up more than half of its land to neighboring countries. The

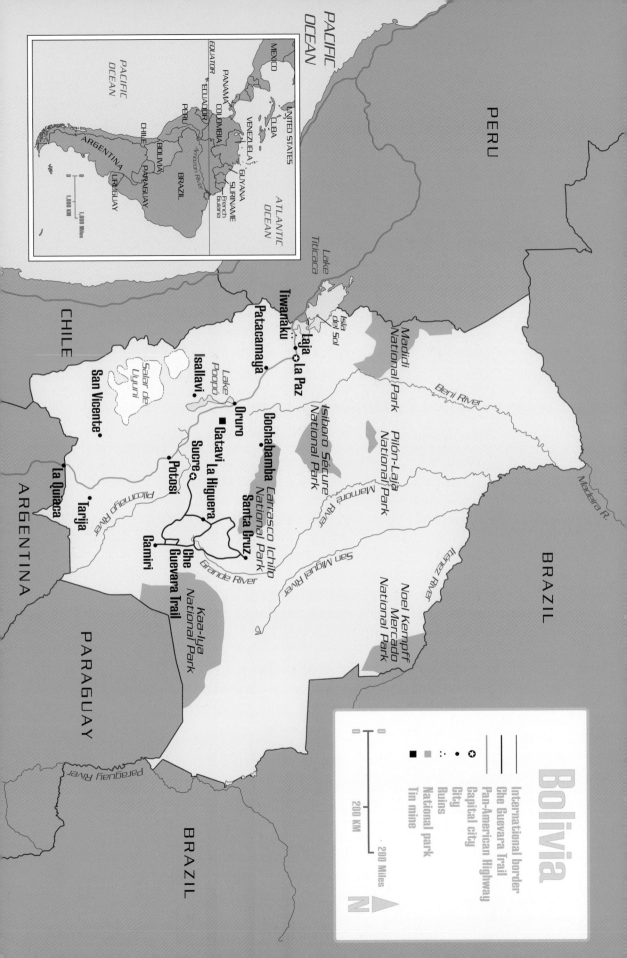

War of the Pacific (1879–1883) was especially devastating. It led to Bolivia losing control of its coastal land, which it needed for trade.

The country's rugged terrain and sparse population limited its economic development. The Andes, however, are rich in minerals, and Bolivia became one of the world's leading producers of tin. Bolivian farmers grew coffee, cacao for chocolate, and the coca plant. Chewing the painkilling coca leaf and drinking coca tea is an ancient tradition in Bolivia. In modern times, it is the main ingredient in the illegal drug cocaine.

Besides physical barriers, cultural barriers between Bolivia's social classes also hampered the country's development. Almost two-thirds of the population was indigenous, or native, peoples. They scratched out their livings as small-scale farmers or endured the brutality of working in the mines. The upper classes—mostly of Spanish descent—denied the working classes voting rights and schooling. Without education, most Bolivians were not involved in running their own country.

The Revolution of 1952 began democratic and social reforms. One dozen years later, however, the military again seized power. Civilian rule came back in 1982. Economic reforms stabilized the economy but widened the gap between rich and poor. At this time, much of Bolivia's coca crop was exported to cocaine-making countries, especially Colombia. The United States and other countries that struggle with cocaine abuse began to pressure Bolivia to wipe out coca growing.

In the twenty-first century, demonstrators took to Bolivia's streets protesting poverty and the lack of equal rights for all. Citizens elected Evo Morales president in December 2005. He is the country's first indigenous president, and he promises to end discrimination against native peoples. Morales supports farmers' rights to grow coca for uses other than making cocaine. His government has also taken the natural gas industry and other important resources under its control. Not all Bolivians support Morales's controversial moves. But the nation hopes to improve Bolivia's status, which ranks as the poorest country in South America.

THE LAND

The Republic of Bolivia lies in the heart of the South American continent. With an area of 425,000 square miles (1.1 million square kilometers), Bolivia is about the size of Texas and California combined. The nation's neighbors include Brazil to the north and east, Paraguay to the southeast, and Argentina to the south. On the west, Chile and Peru block Bolivia's access to the Pacific Ocean, making Bolivia a landlocked nation.

▶ Topography

Three regions make up Bolivia's topography, or landscape. The Andes Mountains region of western Bolivia consists of two Andes mountain chains cutting across Bolivia. A high mountain plain sits between the mountain chains. The land descends from the peaks into the Sub-Andean region. The broad valleys of this region enjoy a moderate climate, where forests thrive. Bolivia's Lowlands region stretches eastward from the mountains and valley. The landscape of the Lowlands varies from rain forest to grassland to scrubland.

ANDES MOUNTAIN REGION The Andes Mountains dominate this region of highlands. The Andes is the world's longest mountain chain. It runs the entire length of South America—about 4,500 miles (7,240 km)—and reaches its widest point in Bolivia. Volcanic eruptions over the past 65 million years formed the Andes. Volcanic ash created fertile soil on the mountain slopes.

Bolivia's Andean peaks tower to heights of more than 20,000 feet (6,100 m). The Cordillera Occidental (Western Range) forms the border with Chile. To the east is the Cordillera Oriental (Eastern Range). It is also called the Cordillera Real (Royal Range).

Between the ranges is a 12,000-foot-high (3,658 m) plateau, or elevated plain. It is called the altiplano, which means "high plain" in Spanish. The altiplano averages only 80 miles (129 km) in width. It runs 500 miles (800 km) north and south. Mountains on either side block rain from reaching the dry altiplano.

Living at high altitudes is not easy because of the cold weather and

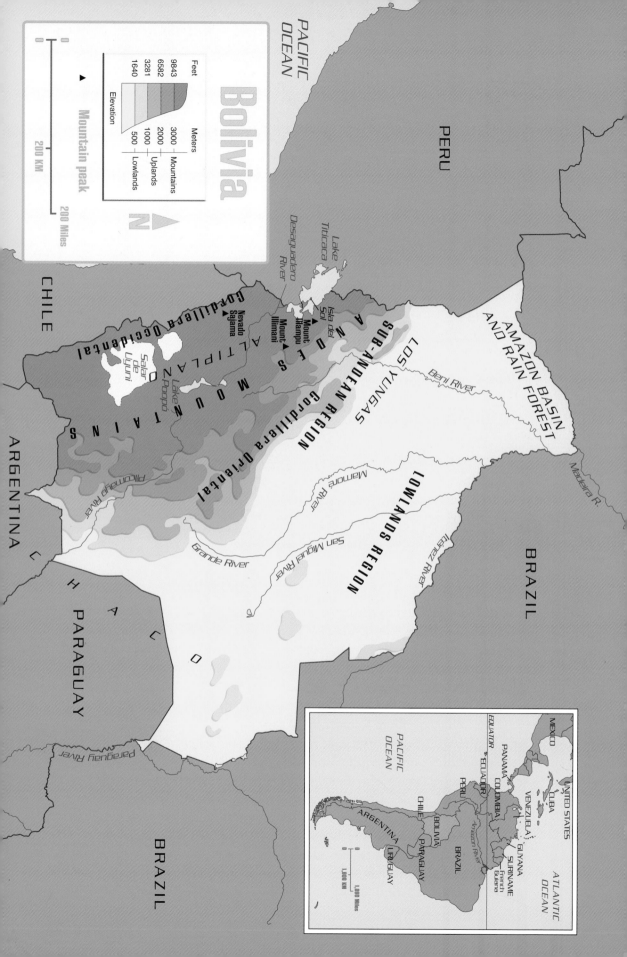

Mount Illimani rises high above La Paz.

the lack of oxygen in the air. Nevertheless, about half of Bolivia's population lives on the altiplano, many in the capital city of La Paz. Mining is important employment on the altiplano. At the highest elevations, herders raise sheep and llamas.

On Bolivia's border with Peru sits Lake Titicaca, one of the world's highest lakes. It is the traditional homeland of the indigenous Aymara people. *Titicaca* means "gray puma" in the Aymara language. Fishing crews harvest fish from the lake, and farmers till its fertile shores.

Snow-topped mountains rise skyward for thousands of feet from their bases on the altiplano. Three mountain peaks in western Bolivia rank among the highest in the world. Bolivia's highest peak is Nevado Sajama, an extinct volcano, which rises 21,464 feet (6,542 m). Mount Illampu peaks at 21,067 feet (6,421 m). The third-highest mountain, Mount Illimani (21,005 feet, or 6,402 meters high), looms over La Paz, Bolivia's largest city.

THE CROWNS OF ILLIMANI

The jagged peaks of Mount Illimani look like the outline of a crown against the sky. This distinctive shape appears on the city seal of La Paz. It also shows up on Bolivian postage stamps, beer labels, and chocolate-bar wrappers.

THE SUB-ANDEAN REGION South and east of the central chain, the Andes begin to descend into the broad upper valleys and hills of the Sub-Andean region. Lying at 10,000 feet to 14,500 feet (3,000 m to 4,400 m) above sea level, the region enjoys a pleasant climate. The valleys surrounding the city of Cochabamba provide the country with most of its food.

Lower, at 2,000 feet to 6,500 feet (600 m to 2,000 m), are semitropical valleys called *yungas*, the Aymara word for "warm." The yungas are to the northeast of the Cordillera Oriental. Few people live here, but

Bolivians in search of natural beauty visit popular resorts in the region. They enjoy the area's steep hillsides; deep, narrow canyons; and thick mountain forests. The yungas' forests also provide many commercially valuable trees.

LOWLANDS REGION The vast Lowlands region east of the Andes is also called the Oriente, which means "east." It covers 70 percent of Bolivia. Rivers from the Andes bring water to the region.

The Lowlands plain, or llano, has three subregions. In the north is part of the tropical Amazon rain forest, which extends into Brazil. It forms the southern edge of the vast Amazon Basin that extends into Brazil. Wetlands here include marshes, river forests, and lagoons. Drier forests and grass-lands, or pampas, cover the east and south Lowlands. In the south-east, a harsh land called the Chaco extends into Paraguay. Few people live in the Chaco's scattered forests or on the poor soils of its scrubland.

Lowland farmers produce sugarcane, rice, and cotton on the plains. Cattle graze on grasslands. The development of a natural gas industry in the 2000s spurs population growth and development, especially around Santa Cruz. Coca production also provides income.

◉ Lakes and Rivers

Lying partly in Bolivia and partly in Peru, Lake Titicaca is the second-largest lake in South America. It covers an area of 3,200 square miles (8,288 sq. km). At 12,507 feet (3,812 m) above sea level, it is the high-est lake in the world that commercial boats can travel on. The lake is 122 miles (196 km) long and 45 miles (72 km) wide. Many bays and coves indent its shoreline. Its blue waters are unusually clear and sink to 75 feet (23 m) deep. The lake contains thirty-six islands, including the large Isla del Sol (Island of the Sun).

When a giant prehistoric lake dried up, the salt in the water settled onto the ground. This created the Bolivian salt flats called Salar de Uyuni.

Water from Lake Titicaca flows through the Desaguadero River southeast to Lake Poopó, which is 500 feet (150 m) lower. One large island sits in Lake Poopó. The lake is extremely salty, and few people live on its shores. South of the lake are the salt flats of Salar de Uyuni. Much larger than Lake Poopó, the salt-covered basin covers about 7,500 square miles (19,425 sq. km). Over the centuries, Bolivians have collected tons of salt from the salt deserts.

Bolivia's rivers rise in the Andes, fed by the melting snow high up in the mountains. The rivers flow northward and eventually reach the Madeira River of Brazil. This river, in turn, empties into the mighty Amazon River. The Beni, Mamoré, Grande, San Miguel, and Iténez rivers are just a few of the rivers in Bolivia that feed into Brazil's Madeira River. Plans are in place to widen and deepen the Paraguay River in order to improve Bolivia's access to the Atlantic Ocean. Smaller rivers, such as the Pilcomayo, drain southeastern Bolivia.

Climate

Bolivia is located in the tropics—the region of Earth near the equator. Its location in the Southern Hemisphere (south of the equator) means Bolivia's seasons are the opposite of the seasons in the Northern Hemisphere. Most Bolivians live at altitudes where the climate is much colder than might be expected. The highest peaks of the Andes are never free of snow. On the altiplano, the air is clear and it is generally cool and dry. The temperature averages 55°F (13°C) in January and 40°F (4°C) in July. Nighttime temperatures drop well below freezing year-round. Strong winds sometimes whip up dust and make the dry air uncomfortable.

In contrast, the climate of the yungas is warm and humid. Temperatures in the valleys average 72°F (22°C) in January and 52°F (11°C) in July. Most of the northern and eastern Lowlands are warm and humid year-round. The average daily temperature there is 75°F (24°C). In the southern Lowlands, dry, cool winds from Antarctica called *surazos* can bring sharp drops in temperatures during June to September.

In most regions of Bolivia, summer (December to March) is the rainy season. The driest parts of the Andes receive only 10 inches (25 centimeters) of rain a year, creating desert conditions. In the Lowlands, average rainfall is 60 inches (152 cm) yearly. The southern Lowlands' climate is semiarid, with little rain, while farther north, the wettest places receive hundreds of inches every year. Rivers overflow and frequently flood pastures and croplands. May through September is the dry season.

Flora and Fauna

Because of its wide range of climates, Bolivia has more kinds of plants than most countries in the world. Woods and forests cover 53 percent of Bolivia. Vast forests grow on the slopes of the Andes and the northern Lowlands. Experts estimate that 1 square mile (2 sq. km) of rain forest is home to 1,200 kinds of plants and 600 kinds of trees. Tree species include the giant kapok and the Brazil nut. The forest's dense canopy, or rooftop, blocks light from reaching the forest floor. Lianas, or woody vines, climb up tree

The **Amazon rain forest** has four levels, and each level supports different ecosystems. The levels are the shady ground, the dim lower tree branches, the sunny canopy, and the tops of the tallest trees.

trunks to reach the sunlight. Orchids, ferns, and mosses live high up in tree branches. Some rain forest plants are the source of valuable medicines. Fishing crews harvest a tropical plant called barbasco for fishing. The plant gives off a drug that paralyzes fish, making them easy to collect.

Grasses and small shrubs comprise the lowland pampas, and cotton grows wild in eastern Bolivia. Small groups of palms and deciduous (leaf-shedding) trees serve as nesting sites for birds. The Chaco's dry climate supports few plants except thorny shrubs, grasses, and cacti. Hatmakers weave the fronds of dwarf palm trees in the area to make traditional hats.

Scanty trees and scrub grasses survive in the dry, rocky Andes. The Andean khantuta flower is Bolivia's national flower. Its red, green, and yellow colors are the colors of the flag. Drought-resistant eucalyptus trees and cacti survive in sheltered places. The native tubers (roots), potatoes, and oca have provided people's main source of food on the altiplano for centuries. Totora reeds from Lake Titicaca's shores provide lake dwellers with materials for mats and boats.

The Andean condor is the national bird of modern Bolivia. The people of the Andean highlands have respected this huge vulture for thousands of years. With a wingspan of more than 9 feet (3 m), the condor is the largest flying bird in the world. It is an important figure in early native mythology, and catching a condor was proof of manhood for young men. The title of the leader of an indigenous community is *mallku*, which means "condor" in the Aymara language.

Animals native to Bolivia include the llama, alpaca, guanaco, and vicuña. These animals are all camelids, or humpless relatives of the camel. Andean people domesticated llamas more than four thousand years ago. Weavers value alpacas for their light and warm fleece, once known to the Incas as the fiber of the gods. Guinea pigs are also native to the Andes. Domesticated guinea pigs are a source of meat.

Bolivia's tropical forests are home to a huge variety of animals. Some animals, such as sloths, spend their lives in trees. Many kinds of monkeys use their tails to move among treetops. Howler monkeys' deep, howling calls can be heard as far as 2 miles (3 km) away in the forest. Pumas, jaguars, wildcats, coatis (related to the raccoon), and anteaters roam the forest floor.

The rain forests of the Amazon Basin are home to thousands of different animal species, including the **Geold's monkey.** The nutrient-rich river water supports unique plants such as **giant water lilies.**

Swamp deer live in marshy lowlands, along with tapirs. Sometimes called the South American elephant, tapirs look like large pigs with short, stubby trunks. Up to 4 feet (1 m) long, capybaras are the world's largest rodents. People eat these riverbank dwellers. The spectacled bear is named for the yellow facial markings on its shaggy black coat. It lives among the wooded foothills of the Bolivian Andes. Bony-plated shells protect armadillos.

Many alligators, lizards, and turtles lurk in the warm, tropical Lowlands along with numerous snakes—including poisonous pit vipers and giant boa constrictors. Hundreds of kinds of fish swim in the slow, muddy Lowlands rivers. They include piranhas, stingrays, and electric eels. The rivers are also home to river dolphins and giant otters.

Majestic Andean condors and eagles soar in Bolivia's mountains. Many kinds of hummingbirds are found in the mountains. Rheas, or South American ostriches, and a species of large stork live in the tropical plains and valleys. The rain forests abound with brightly colored parrots, macaws, and toucans.

Natural Resources

Bolivia has ample natural resources of minerals, land, and water. Zinc has passed tin and gold as Bolivia's leading mineral export, though Bolivia remains one of the world's leading producers of tin. Hydrocarbons—oil and natural gas—are the source of Bolivia's greatest mineral wealth. The mining industry also exports copper, iron, lead, and more.

About 10 percent of Bolivia's land is farmable. Historically, most Bolivians have been farmers. The country's varied topography allows farmers to cultivate many kinds of products. Coffee thrives at high altitudes, while the warm Lowlands of Bolivia supply valuable trees.

Dams on Bolivia's rivers harness the power of rushing water to produce electricity. With irrigation, or artificial watering systems, water is diverted to drylands to aid crop production.

⊙ Environmental Issues

Workers since colonial times have cleared Bolivia's forests to grow crops. The tropical soil, however, has only enough nutrients to support crops for a short while. Then more forest must be destroyed. The international demand for tropical timber also contributes to deforestation, or the loss of woodlands. Poor farming methods, such as overgrazing animals, lead to soil erosion. Desertification then threatens the land. Desertification occurs when soil dries up and wind or rain blows or washes it away.

Pollution is another issue for Bolivia. The development of industries helps the country's economy. But industrial wastes pollute the nation's air and water.

Bolivia protects its environment with almost twenty national parks and protected areas. On the border with Brazil, the Noel Kempff Mercado National Park is Bolivia's largest park. The government named it after a famous Bolivian scientist. Despite protection, fifty-four animal species and seventy plant species face extinction, or are in danger of dying out completely.

Visit www.vgsbooks.com for links to websites with additional information about Bolivia's natural resources. Take an online tour of Noel Kempff Mercado National Park and view pictures of Bolivia's beautiful landscapes and unique landmarks.

⊙ Cities

About 63 percent of Bolivians live in cities. Bolivia has two capital cities. La Paz is the administrative capital. It houses most government agencies. Sucre is the judicial capital and houses Bolivia's Supreme Court.

SANTA CRUZ (population 1.5 million) passed La Paz as Bolivia's largest city in the twenty-first century. Its growth is mainly due to new farms

and the booming oil and natural gas industries. Santa Cruz also profits from the coca trade, although officials have joined with the United States in trying to stamp out the illegal sale of coca for cocaine production. Situated in the middle of fertile, tropical farmlands, the city is hot and humid during much of the year. Most of Santa Cruz's residents are of European descent.

LA PAZ (population 800,500) is Bolivia's second-largest city, though the population of the larger metropolitan area equals Santa Cruz's. The Spanish founded the city in 1548 and named it Nuestra Señora de La Paz (Our Lady of Peace). La Paz is the administrative capital, where the president and Congress work. It is also the chief commercial center of Bolivia.

La Paz is situated at an elevation of 12,000 feet (3,658 m). In the thin, clear air, the people of La Paz can see the snowcapped Andean peaks in the distance. The air is so thin that La Paz does not even have a fire department because there is not enough oxygen in the air for flames to spread.

The population of the city is about evenly divided between people of Aymara or Spanish descent. La Paz is a mixture of historic colonial

In the city of **La Paz,** streets and buildings at the city's center light up at night.

neighborhoods and modern residential areas where well-to-do people live. The Aymara generally live in metal-roofed huts on the steep land on the outskirts of town.

The center of city life is the main square, Plaza Murillo. It boasts the Presidential Palace, the legislative building, and a magnificent cathedral, all facing formal gardens. The University of San Andrés is located in the heart of the city. Performers present concerts and plays in its large outdoor arena.

COCHABAMBA (population 517,000) lies on a fertile plateau midway between Santa Cruz and La Paz. Cochabamba is typically Spanish in layout. A cathedral church dominates its central plaza. Buildings with arcades surround this central square. The cultural life of the city revolves around the University of San Simón.

SUCRE (population 292,000), Bolivia's constitutional, or judicial, capital lies high in the mountains. It is about 260 miles (418 km) southeast of La Paz. Founded in 1538 as Chuquisaca, the city took its current name in 1826 to honor General Antonio José de Sucre. He helped to end Spanish rule in South America.

Sucre is famous for its colonial architecture. The United Nations declared the city a World Heritage Site. Important buildings include the ornate palace where Bolivia's Declaration of Independence was signed in 1825. The city takes pride in the University of San Francisco Javier, founded in 1624. It is one of the oldest universities in the Americas. The city depends on the local oil refinery and cement plant, as well as on farms and factories.

HISTORY AND GOVERNMENT

Scientists believe that the first people in the Americas traveled on a land bridge from Asia to North America about twenty-five thousand years ago. These indigenous Americans, or Indians, eventually migrated to South America. By studying the remains of humans and animals, scientists discovered that people lived in the area of present-day Bolivia at least ten thousand years ago.

▷ Early Civilizations

The prehistory of Bolivia's people is little known. They did not use writing systems, and many difficult-to-reach ancient sites remain unexplored. Evidence shows that early peoples settled in villages. They lived by fishing and farming. In the Highlands, people domesticated llamas and alpacas and hunted wild animals. Farmers grew corn and potatoes and raised guinea pigs for meat.

Beginning about 500 B.C., the Tiwanakans—the first known residents of the area—settled on the south shore of Lake Titicaca. The

civilization reached its peak in about A.D. 900. At that time, about fifty thousand people lived in the city of Tiwanaku. A royal family oversaw an empire whose paved roads linked farming communities. The roads ran west to the coast and east into the valleys below.

Huge stone Tiwanakan ruins attest to a civilization with good engineering skills. Builders cut and ground stones weighing more than 100 tons (91 metric tons) to a smooth finish. The most impressive ruin is an enormous gateway, known as the Gate of the Sun. Nearby, a large carving depicts the sun god carrying a double staff and overseeing an army of forty-eight lesser figures. Other structures nearby may have been temples. They give proof of a civilization with centralized political and religious rule.

Many small indigenous kingdoms or nations arose alongside the Tiwanakan Empire. The inhabitants spoke a language called Aymara and are the ancestors of Bolivia's Aymara people. The shores of Lake Titicaca became the homeland of the largest and most powerful Aymara nations.

Meanwhile, the native people of eastern Bolivia mostly lived in small villages along rivers and in the rain forest. They cut down and burned patches of the thick jungle for farmland. Cassava, a root crop also called manioc or tapioca, provided their main food. They fished and hunted with spears and blow darts for meat.

A *bolas* is an ancient weapon, which various Indian groups in the Chaco area used. It consists of three heavy balls, usually made of stone, joined on long strips of leather. It is thrown with a spinning motion to entangle the legs of prey.

The Tiwanakans disappeared for an unknown reason about A.D. 1200, long before the Incas took over the area. The most probable reason is a long and widespread drought.

◉ The Inca Empire

According to tradition, Manco Capac and his sister-wife, Mama Ocllo, founded the Inca Empire in the thirteenth century A.D. They began a dynasty of family rule that would last nearly five hundred years. The Incas ruled from Cuzco in southern Peru. Their social system balanced the needs of the central government with the needs of local authorities. Each year, for example, officials of the central government estimated the amount of land needed to raise food. They then gave a parcel of land to each family. The state kept the rest of the land. The Inca peasants had to farm this state land before working on their own plots. They grew crops native to the Andes including corn, potatoes, oca, and quinoa (a grain).

Although they lacked modern tools, the Incas were master builders. Ruins of an elaborate system of roads, irrigation tunnels to move water, and terraced mountain slopes still exist. The construction of such public works requires knowledge of advanced math. Learned engineers must have overseen projects built by large numbers of workers.

During the fifteenth century, the Incas began a campaign of military expansion. Within a hundred years, they ruled an empire. It stretched 2,500 miles (4,020 km) along the west coast and Andean region of South America. By 1500 the Incas had conquered peoples of differing languages and customs, including the Aymara. The civilization included between 5 million and 10 million people. Imposing their customs and language, Quechua, the Incas united the different people into one of the world's great empires. The Highlands of present-day Bolivia made up the Inca province of Kollasuyo. The Incas never conquered the scattered peoples living in the Lowlands east of the Andes, however.

The Spanish Conquest

In 1527 Spaniards Francisco Pizarro and Diego de Almagro set sail from present-day Panama in Central America. They were in search of the fabled riches of the Andes. Upon finding gold ornaments everywhere in northern Inca lands, Pizarro returned to Spain to organize the conquest of the Incas. At the time, the Inca Empire was weak due to a bloody civil war. The dispute had begun between two brothers, Atahuallpa and Huáscar. They disagreed over which of them would succeed their father, the Lord Inca, to the throne.

The Spanish conquest of the Incas began in 1532, when Pizarro returned with almost two hundred soldiers. He and his men brought with them horses and guns, which the Incas did not have. By this time, Atahuallpa had killed Huáscar. The Spaniards promised to meet with the victorious brother. Instead, they ambushed him and took him captive. The Incas paid a huge treasure in gold and silver to ransom their leader. The Spanish received 13,420 pounds (6,087 kilograms) of gold and 26,000 pounds (11,800 kg) of silver. Nevertheless, the conquistador, or conqueror, Pizarro ordered Atahuallpa executed. The small Spanish force, with their superior weapons and ruthless organization, then took control of the leaderless Inca Empire.

The Colonial Era

In 1538 the Spanish conquerors established the large colonial empire called the Viceroyalty of Peru. They located the seat of

BEGGAR ON A THRONE

Spanish colonial leaders viewed Upper Peru as a source of silver and gold, mined by forced labor. The leaders ignored Bolivia's social needs and did not invest in long-term developments. The practice set the pattern for Bolivia's history of poverty, despite its ample resources, and led to the description of Bolivia as "a beggar on a throne of gold."

This gold mask depicts the Inca god Viracocha. The Incas believed that Viracocha created their civilization.

Spanish power in Lima, Peru. Spanish viceroys (representatives of the king) in Lima included the land of Bolivia as part of the empire. They called the land Upper Peru (Alto Peru in Spanish). Also in 1538, the Spanish founded Chuquisaca (Sucre) as Upper Peru's capital city.

Early during Spanish rule of Upper Peru, silver was discovered in huge quantities near Potosí. This event had far-reaching consequences for the native peoples. The Spaniards forced large numbers of them to work underground in the mines. The miners chewed painkilling coca leaves to help them bear the constant hunger and hard work in the dark, cold mines. Thousands of them died every year from the brutal conditions.

The period of peak silver production lasted from 1572 to 1630. During this era, the value of the output of the mines at Potosí often exceeded seven million silver pesos (Spanish coins) annually. Potosí became famous for its fabulous riches. It supplied about 70 percent of the mineral exports of the Viceroyalty of Peru.

In the meantime, the Spanish developed huge haciendas (plantations). Under a system called *encomienda*, the Spanish colonial government gave colonists legal rights to use the indigenous people as paid workers. The colonists were supposed to educate their workers in the Roman Catholic religion of Spain. In practice, however, landowners seized land and used the native people as slaves. Landowners also imported a smaller number of Africans as slaves during colonial times.

European diseases, such as smallpox and measles, and harsh treatment killed many indigenous peoples. For the most part, the Indians endured miserable lives under Spanish colonial rule. Many harbored deep anger and hatred against their exploiters.

In the late 1700s, a series of Indian rebellions broke out. Tupac Amarú II (José Gabriel Condorcanqui) was a descendant of the last Lord Inca. He and Tupac Katari (Julian Apaza) led the Aymara peoples of the Andes in a movement to drive out the Europeans and to reestablish self-rule. Tupac Katari, with a force of nearly eighty thousand Aymara, besieged La Paz for more than one

IT'S WORTH A POTOSÍ

In 1545 a native man named Huallpa discovered what would become the richest silver mine in the New World in the area of Potosí. The mines provided enormous wealth for Spain in the colonial era. In modern Spain, when someone wants to describe something extremely valuable, they still say, "It's worth a Potosí." The phrase comes from the famous Spanish novel *Don Quixote* (1615) by Miguel de Cervantes.

In 1590 an artist drew this picture of Indian workers in a silver mine at **Potosí.** Spanish colonists forced them to do this dangerous work without pay.

hundred days in 1781. The Spaniards finally crushed the revolution and executed the leaders.

The War of Independence

The indigenous peoples were not alone in desiring independence from Spain. South American–born people of Spanish descent, called Creoles, wanted freedom too. Spanish-born people held a superior place in society and discriminated against Creoles. The Creoles resented this, and they also wanted to take control of the silver trade.

The successful American and French revolutions of the late 1700s inspired many South Americans to seek their independence. When French emperor Napoleon Bonaparte invaded Spain and overthrew the Spanish king in 1808, colonists took advantage of Spain's weakness. On May 25, 1809, the people of the capital city of Chuquisaca revolted against Spain and established their own government. This set in motion an uprising in La Paz two months later, on July 16. Revolution followed in Cochabamba, Oruro, Potosí, and Santa Cruz.

For almost fifteen years, Creoles waged the War of Independence against the Spaniards. Both sides drafted Indians to fight for them. During the course of the fighting, Spanish rule gradually weakened. But it was an outsider who decided the fate of Bolivia and Peru. Their liberator was General Simón Bolívar from Venezuela. After his victories in Venezuela, Colombia, and Ecuador, Bolívar entered Peru and won another victory on the plains of Junín on August 6, 1824. Four months later, Bolívar's lieutenant, General Antonio José de Sucre, won the Battle of Ayacucho in Peru. This battle marked the end of Spanish rule in Bolivia and Peru.

◎ The Republic

On August 6, 1825, Upper Peru became an independent republic. The new nation was twice as large as present-day Bolivia and had a long Pacific coastline. The country named itself Bolivia in honor of the great liberator. General Bolívar wrote a constitution for the nation. Its first Congress ratified the constitution in 1826.

Bolívar ruled Bolivia for six months before handing over his authority to General Sucre. The following year, Sucre was chosen as the country's first president under the new constitution. He served in office for two and a half years. Then he resigned to take part in independence struggles elsewhere.

After a series of short-lived presidencies, Bolivia gained its first Bolivian-born president—Andrés Santa Cruz—in 1829. He was the

son of a Spanish official and María Calahumana, a descendant of the Incas. Santa Cruz served as president until 1839. His presidency brought peace and order to Bolivia. His administration oversaw the creation of universities at La Paz and Cochabamba, as well as colleges of medicine and science. Lawmakers passed new penal, civil, mining, and commercial codes. Santa Cruz reorganized the nation's finances and encouraged trade and manufacturing.

Simon Bolívar

He ordered the nation's first census and had Bolivia's first general map drawn. Under his rule, an impressive road-building program began. It included the construction of bridges over difficult mountain passes.

Santa Cruz's goal was to become the head of a confederation, or union, combining both Peru and Bolivia. But the governments of Argentina and Chile supported the Peruvians in opposing Santa Cruz. All three countries combined forces to defeat Bolivian troops at the Battle of Yungay in 1839. Thus ended Santa Cruz's dreams of confederation. The Chileans imprisoned him and later exiled him to France, where he died.

Losing Land and Sea

The defeat at Yungay marked the beginning of forty years of strife and uprisings in Bolivia. Seven new national constitutions would come and go during these years. Bitter feuds arose among military officers, landowners, and mine owners. In trying to gain power for themselves alone, these groups paralyzed the national economy. They also deepened divisions among Indians, whites, and cholos (mestizos, or those of mixed Indian-and-Spanish bloodlines). The rivalries did nothing to further Bolivia's sense of itself as a united nation. Reportedly, the ruthless General Manuel Belzu (1808–1866) even said that Bolivia was totally incapable of being governed.

To resolve Bolivia's lack of unity, military officers tried to build a sense of national purpose by taking on foreign foes. The idea was to draw Bolivians' attention away from problems at home. This course proved disastrous for Bolivia. It eventually led to the loss of more than half of the nation's territory.

During the War of the Pacific (1879–1883) among Peru, Chile, and Bolivia, Bolivia lost to Chile the mineral-rich lands along the

THE COST OF BIRD DROPPINGS

Seabird excrement was one of the causes of the War of the Pacific. European nations seeking to feed their fast-growing populations demanded more and more fertilizer for farming. In the mid-1800s, British scientists discovered that the huge deposits of guano—seabird droppings—on Bolivia's Pacific coast contained nitrates, a source of fertilizer. Peru and Chile both leased coastland from Bolivia, where few Bolivians lived. Those countries proceeded to reap riches from selling the guano. When Bolivia tried to tax the guano, Chile's army moved in and took over Bolivia's coast.

Pacific coast. Even worse, it lost access to the Pacific Ocean, making it dependent on Chile and Peru's ports for trade. Bolivians never accepted this loss or had easy relations with Chile afterward.

Meanwhile, Brazilians were settling Bolivia's jungle state of Acre, along the Brazilian–Bolivian border. They were developing rubber tree plantations. Demand for rubber soared at the turn of the twentieth century, as developed nations demanded rubber for tires and industrial use. Because it brought great wealth, the rubber tree earned the nickname *arbol de oro,* which means "tree of gold" in Spanish.

In the early twentieth century, two robber outlaws from the United States arrived in Bolivia with a price on their heads. Known as Butch Cassidy and the Sundance Kid, they held up a payroll shipment on its way to pay miners in 1908. The Bolivian army and armed miners—whose pay had been stolen—caught up to them near San Vicente. The two men died in a shootout.

Brazilians and local Bolivians in Acre worked together to declare this rubber-rich state independent from Bolivia. These Bolivians announced their desire to be annexed, or added, to their powerful neighbor, Brazil. In 1903, by the terms of the Treaty of Petropolis, Brazil gained a large chunk of Bolivia with hardly a struggle.

Bolivians grew wiser from this loss, but still lacked strong leadership. The local political scene again fell into turmoil.

The country's fortunes improved only during World War I (1914–1918). Warring European nations increased their demand for Bolivian tin and beef. Tin surpassed silver as Bolivia's main export. Tin cans, invented in the early 1800s, became important as a way to preserve food. Bolivia sold its minerals and meat only to the Allies—Great Britain, France, and eventually the United States. The nation formally broke off relations with Germany in 1917, when a German submarine torpedoed a ship carrying a Bolivian government minister.

◉ The Chaco War and Its Aftermath

The economy of Bolivia continued to boom after the Allies won World War I. This boom was due to foreign-owned companies discovering and developing oil resources in southern Bolivia. But, as in earlier Bolivian history, only a small number of Bolivians shared in the profits of good times. The income mainly went to Creoles of unmixed European ancestry and cholos who had adopted Western ways and reached middle-class status. The majority of Bolivians remained out-

a dictator. He suspended Congress and out-
lawed all activity by political parties. He
also stifled the labor unions who tried to
protect workers' rights. After being
linked to the illegal drug trade, the
brutal dictatorship was overthrown.
García Meza was tried and found
guilty of abuses against human rights
and sentenced to thirty years in prison.

Bolivia holds the
world record for the
most coups. Between
1825 and 1982, control of
the government
changed hands 188
times. Most of the
coups were
bloodless.

Return to Democracy

To reestablish order after García Meza's brutal
dictatorship, Bolivians turned to the aging leaders of the
1952 revolution. Marking the return of democratic, civilian (non-
military) rule, Bolivians reelected Hernán Siles Zuazo in 1982. Victor
Paz Estenssoro became president again in 1985.

At the time, Bolivia's economy was collapsing. The average Bolivian
wage was about six hundred dollars a year, one of the lowest in South
America. The annual inflation rate reached the world record of 22,000
percent. Paz Estenssoro managed to bring this inflation under control.
He also pressured Bolivians to stop growing coca. His administration
invited U.S. troops to help root out the trade in illegal drugs.
Eventually, these efforts cut Bolivia's drug-trade earnings in half.

Under his successor, Jaime Paz Zamora, the government passed
laws meant to encourage other countries to invest in Bolivia. In 1990
the government announced plans to privatize, or to sell state-run companies to private owners. The sales were intended to help the Bolivian
treasury and to increase employment.

These policies continued through the 1990s. They brought inflation
further under control. Foreign investment in the Bolivian economy
increased. In 1992 Bolivia finally gained free access to the Pacific
Ocean again. Peru gave Bolivia free rights to transport trade goods on
a route leading to the seacoast.

In 1993 none of the several candidates running for president won a
majority of popular votes. Therefore, Congress named Gonzalo
Sánchez de Lozado to be the next president. With only 23 percent of
the votes, he had won the largest percent. Sánchez de Lozado continued privatization. He also began a reform of education and the distribution of federal funds to local governments to spend as they needed.

In 1994 changes to the Bolivian constitution acknowledged that
many ethnic groups and cultures make up the nation. The constitution named the indigenous languages Aymara and Quechua as official

languages, alongside Spanish. It also lowered the voting age from twenty-one to eighteen.

In 1997 General Hugo Banzer Suárez won the presidency, out of a race of ten political parties. Banzer promised to continue reforming the economy as well as the government during his term. He began a "zero coca" plan and ordered special police units to destroy illegal coca crops. Bolivia's supply of coca dropped dramatically. Much of the crop had been exported to cocaine-making countries, especially Colombia. Many small-scale farmers who depended on coca growing suffered, however. In response, violence flared between coca growers and the military.

Juan Evo Morales Ayma became the leader of the coca grower's union. He strongly defended the farmers' right to grow this traditional crop. He and other coca defenders pointed out that the traditional use of coca was not a problem in Bolivia. They declared that it was the responsibility of other governments to curb cocaine abuse in their own countries.

⊙ Social Unrest and Socialism

As Bolivia entered the twenty-first century, a huge gap still separated the nation's rich and poor people. A small, wealthy, Spanish-descended class controlled the nation's political and economic life. Indigenous groups made up about two-thirds of the population. But racism held them back, and they had little political power. Almost 70 percent of Bolivians lived in poverty, struggling to survive as miners and small-scale farmers and merchants. Discovery of huge natural gas deposits

Street vendors in Cochabamba protest an increase in the price of water in February 2000. **"Water war"** protests shut down the city for days at a time.

offered new opportunities. The discovery also raised new questions about how best to control Bolivia's resources.

Corruption in Banzer's government and job losses due to worldwide economic troubles led to public protests. In 2000 a key protest in Cochabamba centered on plans to sell the water company to a U.S.-based company. Social groups feared the sale would lead to higher prices, making water too costly for the poor. Ownership of the water company remained in Cochabamba. This successful "water war," as it was called, led to more conflicts between the government and social groups. Two major demonstrations brought the country to a halt.

In 2001 Banzer resigned from the presidency, after learning he had cancer. Congress approved Gonzalo Sánchez de Lozado as president again in 2002, with only 22 percent of the vote.

In 2003 riots erupted again in the streets of Bolivia, leading to the deaths of more than ninety people. The anger revolved around the nation's oil and gas industry. Groups called for state control of the country's natural resources. Many people believed that doing business with foreign companies benefited only rich Bolivians. The threat of further bloodshed forced President Sánchez de Lozado to resign. Congress appointed Vice President Carlos Mesa Gisbert to the presidency. But large-scale, violent protests forced him to resign too, in June 2005. A transitional leader ran the government until elections in December 2005.

In the 2005 elections, for the first time since the 1952 revolution, Bolivians gave one candidate more than half of their votes. Juan Evo Morales Ayma, the Aymara leader of the coca growers, won 54 percent of the votes. He became the first indigenous president of Bolivia. During his campaign, Morales had promised to change Bolivia's political system to give equality and justice to the nation's poor and indigenous peoples.

THE PINK TIDE

President Morales, a Socialist, is not alone in his political views. In the twenty-first century, many Latin American countries have elected leftist leaders. But while these democratically elected leaders care about leftist causes such as social equality, they are not usually as extreme as revolutionaries of the past. (Fidel Castro's 1959 Communist revolution in Cuba, for instance, led to severe limitations on economic and personal freedoms.) Instead, many Latin leftists tend to look to Europe for moderate Socialist models. Red is traditionally the symbolic color of Communism. Some observers call the wave of left-wing political change in Latin America a pink—not red—tide.

President **Evo Morales** speaks to the press after a 2006 meeting with Spanish Prime Minister Jose Luis Rodriguez Sapatero. The two leaders met in Madrid, Spain.

THE STRIPY SWEATER

President Morales became famous on his 2006 visit to Europe for wearing a striped pullover sweater instead of a suit when he met with leaders. He said that his choice of the sweater was an accident. As he was leaving Bolivia, where it was warm, he recalled that it would be cold in the Northern Hemisphere. So he went back in the house and grabbed the first piece of warm clothing he saw—a stripy sweater.

Morales is a member of the Movement Toward Socialism (Movimiento Al Socialismo—MAS) party. As a Socialist, he believes the state should control the nation's resources. Therefore, Morales began to bring foreign-owned companies under state ownership. His government nationalized oil and gas resources. Bolivia thus can earn higher prices, especially for its important natural gas exports. The nation has the second-largest natural gas reserves known in South America, after Venezuela. Morales works closely with President Hugo Chavez of Venezuela.

Rising earnings from natural gas help Bolivia's growth and social welfare. But nationalization also scares off foreign investment, which the country needs. A former coca grower himself, Morales also legalized coca growing for traditional uses and medicine.

◉ Government

Following its 1967 constitution, Bolivia's executive, legislative, and judicial branches of government share power. Executive power is vested in a president. Since 1952 all adult Bolivians have been eligible to vote. Since 1994 the voting age has been eighteen or older. Voters directly elect the president and vice president to a single five-year term. The president appoints a cabinet of advisers to help guide the government.

Legislative authority is in the hands of a bicameral (two-house) National Congress. It consists of the Chamber of Senators and the Chamber of Deputies. Congress meets once a year for a ninety-day session. The people elect senators and 70 of the 130 deputies to serve six-year terms. The other 60 deputies are chosen by proportional representation from political party lists. Elections for one-third of the members occur every two years. The country is divided into nine departments, or states. Each department sends three senators to make up the twenty-seven-member senate.

Citizens elect prefects (governors) to oversee each of Bolivia's nine departments. Elections for prefects were held for the first time in December 2005. Before that, the president appointed prefects. Prefects serve a four-year term. The departments are subdivided into provinces governed by subprefects. Citizens of each city also elect a mayor and a city council.

Although Sucre is the judicial and legal capital of Bolivia, the seat of government is in La Paz. All legislative and executive functions occur in La Paz. The Supreme Court meets in Sucre. The National Congress appoints judges to serve on the court for ten-year terms. The judicial branch of government also has one district court in each department. Lower courts try minor cases.

Visit www.vgsbooks.com for links to websites with additional information about Bolivia's government. Read news and press releases in Spanish and English, tune in national radio stations, and find what you need to know for a visit to Bolivia.

THE PEOPLE

The population of Bolivia is 9.2 million. About two-thirds of the population is indigenous peoples. The population density is 21 people per square mile (8 people per sq. km). The average for Latin America is 71 people per square mile (27 people per sq. km). Bolivia's population is unevenly distributed. The high plateau of the Andes, with its fertile valleys and sloping hillsides, is much more densely populated than the rest of the country. In the southeastern plains, population density is less than 3 people per square mile (less than 1 person per sq. km). About 63 percent of Bolivians live in cities.

Bolivia's population is young. About 39 percent of Bolivia's population is under 15 years of age. The average for South America is 29 percent. With the large number of young women reaching child-bearing age, Bolivia's population will keep growing. The average Bolivian woman will give birth four times in her lifetime, the highest rate in South America. Experts estimate that Bolivia's popula-

tion will reach 12 million by 2025. The government is satisfied with the country's birthrate.

Life expectancy in Bolivia averages 64 years, with a male life expectancy of 62 years and a female average of 66 years. This is low for South America, where people expect to live to 72 years, on average.

The United Nations' Development Program offers the Human Development Index (HDI) as one way to look at a nation's people. The HDI measures human well-being, or the prospects of a person having a long, healthy life with education and a good standard of living. The UN states that it is not a measure of happiness. Key indicators such as life expectancy, literacy, and average income determine the HDI. Lower numbers reflect higher development. The United States ranks 8 out of 177 countries. Spain ranks 20. Bolivia's neighbors rank 34 (Argentina), 43 (Chile), 72 (Brazil), 85 (Peru), and 89 (Paraguay). Bolivia's HDI rank of 114 places it near the development level of Vietnam and South Africa.

◉ Ethnic Groups

Bolivia is the South American country with the largest number of people who define themselves as Indians. Estimates vary, but about 60 percent of Bolivians are of native descent. Cholos, or people of mixed European and Indian ancestry, comprise about 25 percent of the population. Descendants of Europeans make up the other 15 percent.

The indigenous peoples of Bolivia come from different ethnic groups. The Quechua (30 percent of Bolivians) and the Aymara (25 percent) are the largest groups. The Guaraní, who are fewer in number, live in the Lowlands of the east. Along with more than twenty other small groups, they make up about 5 percent of Bolivia's population. Each group speaks a different language, and many Bolivians do not speak Spanish at all.

The Aymara were originally part of a group from north of Cuzco, Peru, who created the Tiwanakan civilization. After the conquest of the Inca Empire, they settled near Lake Titicaca. Though the Aymara and the Quechua have lived in the mountains of Bolivia for centuries, they have never intermixed. The Quechua live throughout the country but settled especially in Cochabamba and Sucre. They are related to the Incas, whose Quechua language linked a number of smaller indigenous groups.

Most indigenous Bolivians who want to gain political or economic power have had to give up ancestral ways, learn Spanish, and adopt Western culture. A movement is working to end racism so that all Bolivians can participate fully in society without giving up their traditions.

Bolivia's mountainous topography has, for the most part, discouraged Europeans—mostly unused to high altitudes—from immigrating to the country. Most of Bolivia's European population are descendants of Spaniards who came during the colonial period. Small numbers of people with African, German, Asian, and Middle Eastern ancestry have also lived in Bolivia for generations.

Cholos and Europeans make up Bolivia's middle and upper classes.

CLIMBING SACRED SUMMITS

In 1998 Bernardo Guarachi of the Aymara people became the first Bolivian and the first indigenous South American to climb Mount Everest, the highest mountain in the world. The mountaineer has also climbed many Andean peaks. The native peoples of the Andes climbed the highest peaks in South America long before the Spanish arrived. They considered the mountains holy. Guarachi honors this belief. He respectfully asks each mountain, including Everest, for permission before he climbs to its summit.

Cholos have adopted Western ways and given up native culture, though they may also speak a native language along with Spanish.

Health

Bolivia has some of the worst health statistics in the Western hemisphere. The government is struggling to improve this situation, but it spends less than 5 percent of its budget on health care. The number of hospitals, clinics, and doctors is low compared to the size of the population. Only about half the population has adequate access to health care. Doctors and nurses train community health-care workers to help meet the needs of rural people.

Indigenous Bolivians whose families have lived at high altitudes for generations have large chests to accommodate their larger lungs. This biological adaptation evolved because there is less oxygen in the air at high altitudes and lungs have to work harder, thus growing bigger.

Many dangerous diseases affect Bolivians, including hepatitis, tuberculosis, and cholera. Parasites cause illnesses such as *chargas*, which causes intestinal disorders and early death from heart attacks. The tropical disease malaria is a problem in warm, wet areas where mosquitoes that carry the disease breed. HIV/AIDS infects 0.1 percent of adult Bolivians.

Many homes in the country have no running water, electricity, or heat. With no sanitary facilities, sewage and garbage contaminate

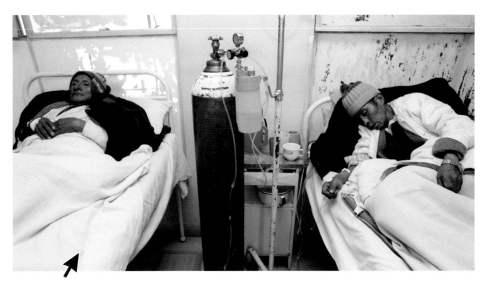

Two miners from Potosí rest in a hospital wing devoted to illnesses such as silicosis, a lung disease caused by inhaling silica dust. Many Bolivian miners do not have access to safety equipment that would protect them from the dust.

MEDICINES AND CHARMS

At markets and fairs, traditional healers sell bundles of leaves, roots, seeds, and resins from sap. They make many of the preparations from plants mixed with fats, powdered bird feathers, hair, and other ingredients. In addition to medicines, the traveling doctor has charms that are believed to solve almost any personal difficulty. Some charms are made of metal or carved stone, bone, or wood. Each one is in the form of a hand holding some object. For example, a hand grasping corn ensures a good corn crop, while a hand grasping money should bring financial success.

A woman sells herbal medicines at a **medicine market** in La Paz. Herbal cures may be chewed, brewed into tea, or packed into a bandage.

drinking water. Boiling water kills germs that spread diseases such as dysentery. But wood and gas for heating water are hard to get. The rural diet is often not very nutritious. Experts estimate that 7 percent of Bolivian children under the age of five and 23 percent of the entire population suffer from malnutrition. Furthermore, many children are not vaccinated against deadly childhood diseases such as measles. For these reasons, many babies die before their first birthday, especially in rural areas. Bolivia's infant mortality rate—54 deaths per 1,000 births—is the highest in Latin America. However, it is a great improvement over Bolivia's 205 deaths per 1,000 infants in 1970.

Few trained physicians visit the Andes region. But a group of traditional healers called traveling doctors use folk cures, natural medicines, and sometimes magic in the Bolivian highlands. They travel long distances in groups of eight or ten, carrying their medicines in woven bags slung over their shoulders. These doctors are said to have influence over the supernatural and spiritual worlds. Patients report that the doctors have performed miraculous cures. Traveling doctors are highly respected.

Some rain forest plants are the source of valuable medicines. Bark of the cinchona tree, for instance, is the source of quinine. This is an important medicine for treating malaria.

Education

Primary education is free for children in Bolivia. The government spends 23 percent of its budget on education. The law requires children to attend school from the ages of six to fourteen. The public schools do not meet the nation's needs, however. Rural children especially lack education. They have to travel long distances to school, and many poor parents keep their children at home to work. About 90 percent of primary-age students attend school, but rural children often go for only a year or two. Less than half of Bolivia's children finish primary school. Of those who do, 87 percent go on to attend secondary school. People who can afford it often pay to send their children to private schools.

Since most young children do not speak Spanish at home, they learn Spanish as a second language at school. Laws require bilingual education for children who do not speak Spanish. The public schools offer Roman Catholic religious instruction, but students are not required to attend the classes.

Young people study at a rural school near the San Cristobal Mine near Potosí. Many boys attend school part-time because they have mining jobs. Some get their first jobs when they are only twelve years old. Many girls also have to work at home instead of attending school.

Ten universities and many private colleges exist in Bolivia. Founded in 1624, the University of Saint Francis Javier in Sucre is one of the oldest universities in the Americas. Students must pass two entrance exams to gain a place at a university.

Despite challenges, the number of Bolivians who can read and write is steadily increasing. About 87 percent of the overall population is literate, or able to read and write basic sentences. This is an improvement over the 63 percent literacy rate of 1994. More girls than boys are kept home from school. Therefore, more men (93 percent) than women (81 percent) can read and write. Literacy is much higher in cities than in rural areas. Among young people, the literacy rate reaches 97 percent.

Daily Life

Bolivia's citizens are divided by class and by a gap between urban and rural dwellers. About 62 percent of all Bolivians live in poverty. The average yearly earnings per person stand at about three thousand dollars, making Bolivia one of the poorest South American countries.

Bolivia's campesinos continue to live off the land. Even with land reform and the distribution of farmland, many Bolivians are unable to raise enough food for their families on poor soil and steep hillsides. The government tries to improve the life of farmers by teaching better ways to till the land and providing improved seed and fertilizers to boost crop production.

Rural Bolivians do their laundry in roadside streams. They spread garments out on the ground to dry in the bright sun. Many women carry their babies on their backs—along with supplies and needlework—wherever they go. People who have small farms live in adobe houses with roofs of thatched straw. Adobe is sun-baked brick made of mud mixed with straw. Those who work in the mines live nearby with their families in huts made of stone and mud.

Bolivians travel Lake Titicaca on canoelike reed boats called balsas. Reeds that grow along the shore provide the material to make the boats. Fishing crews use them daily for fishing, and balsas last for about five months. Usually only two people ride in a balsa, though it can hold as many as four. On short trips, small sails of reed power the balsas. On longer trips, cloth sails are used.

An Aymara man and his son prepare a pair of reed boats, called **balsas,** at the edge of Lake Titicaca.

Most of Bolivia's upper-class citizens live in cities. Although they make up a small percentage of the country's population, the wealthy have traditionally controlled the government and the largest businesses. The well-to-do often send their children abroad for higher education. The life of the urban middle class, which includes cholos as well as European descendants, is in sharp contrast to the lives of the working classes. Those who are financially secure live in much roomier and more comfortable housing, and often they employ servants to help with household work.

Many Aymara live in the capital, La Paz. They frequently know only enough Spanish to trade in the marketplace. Indeed, it is only at the marketplace, one of the liveliest places in the city, that the Aymara interact with the city's wealthier people. At the huge indoor market, the Aymara operate stalls selling vegetables, fruits, meats, and flowers. The women who usually run the stalls knit or weave to pass the long hours, sometimes accompanied by their children. The marketplace is filled with contrasts. For example, llamas from the mountains bear loads of produce and ice, while mules from the Lowlands come bearing oranges and other tropical fruits.

Visit www.vgsbooks.com for links to websites with additional information about the people of Bolivia. Read about the history of the Aymara and Quechua peoples and learn phrases in each of the country's different languages.

CULTURAL LIFE

Unlike most South American countries, Bolivia has never lost its pre-colonial culture. Isolation protected the traditional ways of the indigenous people, who continued to make up the majority of the population.

Major civilizations in Bolivia before the arrival of the Spanish left behind important stone sculptures and ruins, ceramic art, sacred textiles, and gold and silver ornaments. The Spanish settlers introduced their own cultural styles, which developed into a distinctive style of art, architecture, and music during the colonial period. Modern Bolivian artists look to their rich history and the country's vivid folklore. Regional folk music and dances, for instance, are very much alive in the country's annual fiestas, or festivals.

◎ Religion

Roman Catholicism was the state religion during the Spanish colonial era. In modern times, Bolivia has no state religion. The constitution guarantees religious freedom. About 89 percent of Bolivians consider themselves Catholic. Protestant Christianity is the religion of 9 percent of the population. This includes a small but growing number of people who belong to Evangelical Christian denominations. Other Bolivians follow ancient, native religions. Indigenous beliefs and practices sometimes blend with Christian ones. The mixture of religions is called syncretism.

The indigenous beliefs of the Andes region honor a supreme creator god. The Supreme Being is embodied in the gods and goddesses of natural forces, such as wind and rain, the sun, and Earth. The goddess Mother Earth, called Pachamama, holds a special place as the source of life. People are Pachamama's children, and it is their duty to cherish and care for the planet. The mountains also play a central role in traditional Andean beliefs and ceremonies. Worshippers burn offerings such as coca leaves on mountain altars to thank the spirits of the natural world. They believe that this pleases the forces of nature. They hope the forces will respond by providing good weather, bountiful harvests, and security in their daily lives.

Fiestas, Holidays, and Sports

Bolivia has many fiestas throughout the year. Scarcely a week passes when villagers cannot attend a fiesta in their own village or a nearby town. Fiestas celebrate a historical event or a particular Catholic saint, or holy person. The activities, however, may be as much traditional as Christian.

Fiesta dances are largely of Spanish origin, with local elements added. In the mountains, the *cueca*, or handkerchief dance, is the most popular. In this dance, the partners circle round and round one another, linking their arms at intervals—much as in a North American square dance. All the while, they wave a handkerchief in tiny spirals above their heads. People dance the cueca at all major fiestas. Dancing lasts from midmorning until early evening.

Bolivians celebrate May 27 as Mother's Day. On this day in 1812, the women of Cochabamba defended their city against an attack by Spanish soldiers. The city's men had died or were away fighting in the revolutionary war.

Oruro hosts one of South America's best-known festivals, La Diablada, or the Devil Dances. Dancers in masks and costumes act out a struggle between angels and demons. Musicians accompany the dancers on traditional instruments. The weeklong fiesta blends Christian and precolonial traditions to honor the Christian Virgin Mary as well as Pachamama.

All through the year, Bolivians look forward to the excitement of Carnaval, the biggest fiesta. Like Mardi Gras in the United States, it is held just before Lent, a forty-day period of fasting and prayer leading up to Easter. During Carnaval, music and dancing go on for several days. Men wear their best black suits. Women dress colorfully in full skirts and shawls with bright embroidery.

A family wedding is also an occasion for great merrymaking in Bolivia. After the church service, the couple leads the procession to the home of the bride. There a banquet is waiting, paid for by the bridegroom and his parents. A band provides music for dancing. The celebration continues all day and far into the night.

Secular (nonreligious) holidays include New Year's Day (January 1), Labor Day (May 1), and Independence Day (August 6). March 23 is Día del Mar, or Sea Day, when Bolivians remember losing access to the sea to Chile. Each of Bolivia's nine departments also celebrates its founding with a holiday.

Soccer, called *fútbol* (football), is Bolivia's favorite sport. Large crowds turn out to watch their favorite teams compete fiercely.

Bolivia's **Erwin Sánchez (left)** takes the ball from Germany's Matthias Sammer *(right)* during a 1994 World Cup soccer game in the United States. Germany went on to win the game.

Volleyball and basketball are also popular. Visitors and locals climb, hike, and ski in the Andes Mountains.

Literature

Bolivia's precolonial literature was passed down through the generations through plays, oral storytelling, and poetry. There is no written literature from this time, but storytelling still thrives in rural communities. Folktales often involve animal characters. One figure is the trickster—an animal such as a fox who is smaller or weaker than his or her enemies but who survives by wit and cunning. Fantasies and myths of indigenous culture inspire modern Bolivian writers.

Bolivia's colonial Spanish literature was largely made up of historical chronicles and religious works written by priests and administrators. The leading Bolivian writer after independence was Gabriel René-Moreno. He wrote histories, biographies,

TOO-HIGH SOCCER

In 2007 soccer's governing body, the FIFA (the International Federation of Association Football, known by its French initials) banned international soccer games from being played in stadiums higher than 9,800 feet (3,000 m) above sea level. The FIFA stated that the rule is to protect the health of soccer players, who are endangered by the thin air, and to end unfair advantage to soccer players used to the extreme altitude. As a result, La Paz can no longer host soccer games. President Morales spoke out against the ban, and Bolivian demonstrators took to the streets in support of him.

essays, and vivid descriptions of Bolivia's towns and countryside. René-Moreno was a harsh critic of Bolivian politics. He was also prejudiced against native peoples. Nevertheless, modern Bolivians honor him for his contributions to written history.

In the early twentieth century, Adela Zamudio (1854–1928) was a poet who dedicated her life and her writing to ending the oppression of women. Ricardo Jaime Freyre (1866–1933) and Franz Tamayo (1878–1956) were central to the literary scene. Whereas earlier writers had focused on the misery of the native peoples, Tamayo was proud of his native heritage and emphasized its nobility. Known for his poetry, Tamayo also was involved in politics. Bolivian writing focused on the themes of social injustice and the reality of everyday life as the twentieth century progressed. Low literacy rates, however, hampered the development of Bolivian literature.

After the Chaco War, Bolivians awoke to a need for greater unity and nationalism. Writing became more political. Some authors criticized the government. Others, such as Augusto Céspedes and Fernando Ramírez Velarde, dealt with the social issues of poor Bolivians. Céspedes (1904–1997) was a key figure in politics and literature. His novel *Metal del Diablo* (Devil's Metal, 1946) presents the harsh life of tin miners. Javier del Granado (1913–1996) combined storytelling with rural and Quechuan themes. His collections of poems include *Canciones de la Tierra* (Songs of the Earth, 1945).

After the 1952 revolution, social-protest writings either glorified the revolution and its victory or criticized the government for making too few changes. But various dictators in the next decades restricted writers' freedom of expression. In the 1980s, many Bolivian and other Latin American writers turned to magic realism—an experimental way of telling stories, blending reality and fantasy.

Bolivia's first female president, Lidia Gueiler Tejada, is also an author. She published her autobiography, *Mi pasión de lidereza* (My Passion as a Leader), in 2000. Alfonso Gumucio Dagron (b. 1950) is a poet and modern author of more than twenty books on communication, film, and literature. Also a journalist and photographer, he is concerned with the environment and the rights of children and indigenous peoples.

Students at the University of San Andrés in La Paz practice together in an **Aymara language class.** Many choose to study indigenous languages because of interest in their ancestors' lives.

Language

Bolivia has three official languages—Spanish, Quechua, and Aymara. The majority of Bolivians speak Aymara as their native tongue. This language has survived from pre-Inca times. About 40 percent of the population speak Spanish as their native language. It is also the language of government, education, and business. Bolivians who want to succeed in these fields speak Spanish. Most Bolivians speak at least a little Quechua, which was the language of the Incas. In the countryside, Bolivians speak many different languages. When they move to cities, however, people often learn some Spanish.

Bolivia has more local and community radio stations than most countries. They offer a wide variety of local music and news. Bolivians also listen to international stations such as the Voice of America.

Art

Bolivians keep alive a rich tradition of intricately woven textiles, inherited from ancient times. Aymara and Inca artists created beautiful, multicolored clothes for religious and social ceremonies. They spun alpaca and llama fleece into a fine yarn, similar to silk. They dyed cloth with deep, rich colors made from insects and plants.

Symbols and colors are important to Bolivian woven designs, and different communities use different patterns. Images of animals,

A campesino woman dries strands of **llama wool** on the altiplano. She used local plants to dye the wool black and red. Next, it will be spun into yarn.

landscape, and the planets, for instance, have mythical meanings. After the Spanish conquest, artists added horses and Christian symbols. In the Andes, knitters create wool hats and other goods with patterns of llamas, mountains, and geometric designs. Modern artists also create pottery, jewelry, wood carving, and metalwork with a blend of modern and precolonial techniques.

In the twentieth century, modern painters depicted their country's land, landscape, and peoples. The paintings of Cecilio Guzman de Rojas (1899–1950) display his interest in both the Spanish period and the Incas. He painted many portraits of people with Inca features. The 1952 revolution inspired the group of younger artists called the Generation of 52 to renew pride in the nation's culture. Mural painting on walls was one way they reached a wide audience with their ideas about justice for the working classes. Walter S. Romero (b. 1925) and Gil Imana (b. 1933) are the best-known muralists from this time.

Marina Núñez del Prado (1910–1995) was one of Bolivia's—and Latin America's—most famous sculptors. Indian themes, music, the human body, and the animals of the Andes inspired her work. Núñez del Prado's materials include native woods and stone such as black granite and marble. She showed her concern for social issues in works such as *Miners in Revolt* (1946). Working in bronze, she created *Andean Women in Flight* for the 1988 Olympic Games. The National Museum of Art in La Paz showcases contemporary artists, including Roberto Valcarcel (b. 1951).

Music

Bolivian music remains connected to its native roots. Traditional instruments include the *zampona* (reed pipes of various lengths, bound together with colored wool), wooden flutes, and percussion instruments. Musicians also play European violins and guitars.

In the 1960s, Edgar "Yayo" Jofré and his band Los Jairas helped popularize the slow, sad-sounding music of the Andes. Through his and others' efforts, flute-based folk music of the altiplano became popular around the world. Music in Bolivia's east and northeast, on the other hand, employs fast, happy-sounding rhythms.

In the 1980s, the band Los K'jarkas from Cochabamba performed dance music drawing on styles that enslaved Africans had brought to Bolivia. Their music was part of the era's Latin dance craze, the *lambada*.

Modern musicians blend traditional forms with styles from North America and Europe. For instance, some bands perform pop versions of *tinku* music in big-city nightclubs. Tinkus are ritual fighting dances from indigenous communities of the altiplano.

Some unusual Bolivian musical instruments include *chaj'chas*—shakers made from dried sheep hooves. The *charango* is a twelve-stringed guitar originally made from an armadillo shell. Drum makers construct *bombo* drums from hollowed-out tree trunks stretched with llama skin or goatskin.

A Quechua man plays the **pututu,** made from an animal horn, at a ceremony in Sucre. The pututu was originally used by Inca messengers.

> Visit www.vgsbooks.com for links to websites with information about the history of Bolivian art and music. Play samples of the different kinds of Bolivian music, including traditional songs, tinku tunes, and selections from popular groups such as Los K'jarkas.

Clothing

In the cities, Bolivians generally wear Western-style clothing. Children dress neatly to go to school. Many campesinos who move to cities maintain their traditional clothes. The women wear their hair in long braids and a hat. The many kinds of hats include a common, soft rounded derby made of felt (thick wool). Women wear an apron over a full, bright skirt called a *pollera*. Many underskirts help to keep the women warm and make their skirts stand out like hoopskirts. Women frequently wrap a manta—a beautiful, fringed, Spanish shawl—around their shoulders. Their garments are of many bright colors and often include something red. On their backs, they may carry a baby or bundle in a square cloth pack called an *aguayo*. Good-luck dolls made of clay are tucked in with the bundles on their backs.

While the women keep warm with many petticoats and woolen shawls, native men wear a woolen poncho, often a red one. A thick leather belt cinches their shin-length trousers. The men usually wear a *chullo*, or a cap with earflaps,

An Aymara woman knits while waiting with her child at the edge of Lake Titicaca. Bolivia is famous for colorful **knitting,** especially shawls and hats.

Young citizens of La Paz hang out after school. Many young people, especially those who live in cities, follow fashion news from Brazil, the United States, and Spain.

which they often knit themselves. In many regions, campesinos wear leather sandals with soles made out of rubber cut from a used tire.

Food

Potatoes are a staple food in the Andes, since this native vegetable flourishes in high altitudes. There are more than two hundred varieties, including sweet potatoes. In the fertile land around Lake Titicaca, two crops—quinoa and oca—provide other basic foods. Farmers have raised these plants in Bolivia for centuries. Quinoa is a plant with a heavy head of large seeds. After being roasted and boiled, quinoa seed porridge has a pleasant nutlike taste. Oca is a slender root that looks like a small sausage.

Bolivians freeze-dry potatoes and ocas for later use. They spread the vegetables on the ground to freeze at night and to thaw in the sunlight. For several days, they trample the vegetables with their bare feet to squeeze out the moisture. Finally, only the light, dry husk is left. It keeps for a long time. Travelers carry ocas when they go on a long journey, for ocas can be cooked quickly. The preserved potatoes are called *chuño*. They are a main ingredient in stews and soups.

Bolivian families generally eat together. While poor, rural Bolivians eke out a high-starch diet of chuño, ocas, and quinoa, the nation's wealthy can afford meat and fresh fruits and vegetables. A meal for the well-to-do might begin with a hearty chicken soup. Roasted kid (young

Many Bolivian farmers sell their produce at **weekly markets** in the town closest to their farms. This La Paz woman is selling sweet potatoes, onions, tomatoes, and different kinds of peppers from her family's farm.

goat), pork, or beef might follow, along with vegetables in a cream sauce. Cooks also use llama meat dried and preserved but seldom serve it fresh.

Saltenas are popular turnovers with a crust of pizzalike dough. Cooks stuff them with different ingredients, such as a mix of pork or chicken with raisins and chili peppers. Corn is another basic food, prepared in many ways. Young, fresh ears of corn are delicious roasted. *Humitas* is a kind of corn pudding or pie. *Api* is a thick, sweet corn drink. Served hot and spiced with cinnamon, it makes a good breakfast on cold mornings. Some rural people make a corn-based alcoholic drink called *chicha* at home.

For dessert, diners often enjoy fruit from the tropical valleys, such as baked plantain (a type of banana) or fresh papaya. Tropical fruit juices include pineapple, carambola, or star fruit, and sweet-sour tamarind juice.

HUMITAS (BOLIVIAN CORN PUDDING)

Corn pudding is popular in Bolivia and all over South America. Cooks bake it in dried corn husks (the outer leaves of ears of corn), the same way they prepare tamales. This simpler version is cooked in a baking dish. You can add more or less spices, as you like. Bolivians serve this with soup, but it may seem more like a dessert to North Americans.

½ c. milk

4 c. corn (fresh, or thawed frozen kernels)

1½ c. yellow cornmeal

¼ c. raisins

2 tbsp. sugar

1 tsp. salt

½ tsp. baking powder

½ tsp. cinnamon

½ tsp. anise seeds, crushed (optional)

½ tsp. cayenne pepper

3 eggs

1 c. Muenster cheese, shredded

1. Preheat oven to 375°F. Lightly coat a 2-quart baking dish with butter or vegetable oil.
2. In food processor or blender, combine milk with 3 cups of the corn. Blend until smooth.
3. In large bowl, combine cornmeal, raisins, sugar, salt, baking powder, cinnamon, anise seeds (if used), cayenne pepper, and remaining 1 cup of corn. Mix well. Stir in blended milk and corn.
4. In another large bowl, beat the eggs.
5. Gently stir the corn mixture into beaten eggs. Spoon the mixture into the prepared baking dish. Top with Muenster cheese.
6. Bake until golden brown and a toothpick inserted into center comes out clean, about 30 to 40 minutes. Cool for 20 minutes before cutting into squares.

Serves 6 to 8

THE ECONOMY

Bolivia is one of the poorest and least industrially developed countries in South America. Its landlocked position and high altitude have limited trade and development. Agriculture still employs more Bolivians than any other economic endeavor, but it brings in little money. Mining has been the main source of Bolivia's wealth since colonial times. But world demand—and thus world prices—go up and down wildly. Unreliable earnings have led to periods of social unrest in Bolivia. In recent years, exports of oil and natural gas have partly replaced other minerals. The coca leaf is Bolivia's other big money-maker, but it is also politically and socially troublesome.

Debate over who controls Bolivia's natural resources has also led to unrest. Some Bolivians resent foreign companies draining money from their country. Others point out that Bolivia needs foreign investment to pay for development. For instance, it was foreign companies' funding that led to the discovery of natural gas deposits.

Bolivia's economy enjoyed a turnaround in the early 2000s after many

years of high inflation, slow growth, and political instability. Bolivia's annual growth rate of close to 4 percent matches that of most of its neighbors in Latin America. Poverty and widespread unemployment, however, present a major challenge to the government. The unemployment rate is 11 percent overall and far higher in rural areas. The government relies partly on foreign aid and loans to meet its budget needs.

Services and Tourism

Services provide 51 percent of Bolivia's gross domestic product, or GDP, the value of goods and services produced in a country in a year. The service sector offers public and private services rather than producing goods. It includes jobs in government, health care, education, banking, retail trade, transportation, and tourism. About 42 percent of Bolivia's workers hold service jobs. Bolivia's government is a large service employer. It hires medical workers, teachers, laborers, administrators, and more.

THE MOST DANGEROUS ROAD IN THE WORLD

The road *(above)* from La Paz down into the steep valleys of the yungas is known as the most dangerous road in the world. The road plunges at steep angles, and the surface is often rough. Furthermore, large chunks of the mountain regularly fall onto the road.

The road that winds through the yungas is called a **cornice road.** It sticks out from the steep cliffs like the narrow ledges, called cornices, used to decorate buildings.

Bolivia's amazing landscapes and historical cities and ruins attract tourists. It is a special destination for the adventurous who don't mind rough travel over poor roads. More than 300,000 visitors bring close to $300 million to the country every year. Most arrivals come from nearby countries, mainly Peru.

▶ Transportation and Communications

Bolivia has 39,049 miles (62,843 km) of roads, but only 2,343 miles (3,771 km) of them are paved. The Pan-American Highway, which links North and South America, crosses Bolivia. It runs from Peru in the northwest to Argentina in the south. A highway also links Bolivia with the Chilean port of Arica, an important transfer point for Bolivian exports. Railways run for 2,255 miles (3,629 km). Commercial boats can travel waterways for 8,750 miles (14,000 km). Buses serve cities, but few rural Bolivians have access to motorized transportation. One car exists for every thirty-six people. The men often ride mules, but the women walk.

Air transportation is important to Bolivia because of its rough landscape. Bolivia has sixteen airports with paved runways and more than one thousand unpaved airports. Several international and national airlines land at El Alto Airport, the highest commercial airport in the world. Only 5 miles (8 km) from La Paz, El Alto is 12,000 feet (3,650 m) above sea level.

Communications in a country of such rugged terrain have posed problems. The country uses 650,000 telephone landlines, mostly in La Paz. However, cellular phone use is growing rapidly. Bolivians use more than 2.5 million cellular phones.

Radios have long brought news and entertainment to Bolivians, as television reception is poor in rural areas. The country boasts more than 5.5 million radios and more than 300 radio broadcast stations. About 1 million televisions tune in 200 television broadcast stations. Bolivia counts 500,000 Internet users and 9 Internet service providers. Eight national newspapers and many local ones also help keep Bolivians informed.

Industry and Oil and Natural Gas

The industrial sector includes the oil and natural gas industry, mining, and manufacturing. It provides 36 percent of Bolivia's GDP. Jobs in industry employ 14 percent of the nation's workers. Oil and natural gas production is the leading industrial earner. The country produces enough oil and gas to meet its own energy needs.

Bolivia has proven oil reserves of 440 million barrels. The first hint that petroleum lies beneath Bolivian soil appeared in 1895, but oil was not exploited until the 1920s. The control of production, refining, and export of oil has gone back and forth between private investors and the government since then. The issue of who controls this natural resource has generated much political debate and sometimes violence. The government of President Morales began to nationalize the oil industry in 2006. The principal oil fields are in the east and southeast.

A refinery in Cochabamba produces enough gasoline, kerosene, and lubricants for Bolivia's domestic use. Bolivia also exports a share of its production to Argentina and Brazil. Bolivia's construction of a pipeline to Brazil, completed in 2004, became the largest such project in South America.

Huge deposits of natural gas near Santa Cruz were discovered in 1998. Further exploration revealed that in South America, Bolivia's deposits of natural gas are second only to Venezuela's. Natural gas is one of Bolivia's most important exports. A natural gas pipeline connects Santa Cruz to the Pacific coast at Arica, Chile. Natural gas also flows by pipeline to Argentina and Brazil.

Mining

Once Bolivia's largest earners, minerals make up only 10 percent of the country's legal exports. Mines employ about 2 percent of the workforce. It is said that almost every known mineral may be found somewhere in Bolivia. Miners take silver, gold, tin, tungsten, lead, mercury, nickel, antimony, zinc, copper, bismuth, uranium, and iron from the ground. They also mine nonmetallic substances such as asbestos, limestone, mica, salt, and sulfur.

Palliras are women who work independently near mines. They break stones with hammers, looking for bits of metal ore to sell. The existence of such labor-intensive and poorly paid work is a sign of Bolivia's extreme poverty.

Most of Bolivia's mining operations take place in the narrow belt of land that runs from north to south along the Cordillera Oriental. Tin has long been Bolivia's principal mineral asset. The country is the only large-scale source of this metal in the Western Hemisphere. Rugged mountains separate tin mines from points of shipment on the coast. A further handicap is the fact that Bolivia's purest metal ores have already been mined. All of these factors have contributed to the drop of Bolivia's earnings from tin. In the twenty-first century, it ranks behind zinc and gold as a mining export.

Two miners push a cart full of silver ore out of a mine near Potosí. Ore is a mixture of silver and minerals. Miners deliver ore to refineries, which separate the silver from the other substances and prepare it for sale.

Manufacturing

Bolivia has many small manufacturing businesses. Textile manufacturers produce cotton and cotton products. Hydroelectric energy often provides power for cement factories, food-processing plants, shoe factories, and various other industries.

Bolivians continue, however, to rely heavily on imports of manufactured items. The chief imports are food products, mining machinery, medicines, paper products, textiles, and iron and steel products. Because Bolivia has no seaports, its imports and exports pass through ports in Chile and Peru. Goods also come through ports on rivers flowing into the Amazon and the port La Quiaca on the Bolivian-Argentine border.

Many manufactured goods are produced unofficially, out of the sight of the government. Small businesses make clothes, handicrafts, and foods. Many goods are also brought into the country illegally. It is unknown how many Bolivians make a living by smuggling processed consumer goods, but they may number in the thousands.

Agriculture

Agriculture, including forestry and fishing, provides 13 percent of Bolivia's GDP. It continues to utilize most of the nation's workforce, however, with 44 percent of workers.

Bolivia's farmland, like its mines, was once held almost entirely by a few rich families. The injustices, poverty, and hunger resulting from this system helped to spark the revolution of 1952. The following year, a land reform act went into effect. As a result, the campesinos acquired small tracts of land of their own. Old-fashioned methods of farming and lack of education still bind farmers. Most farmers are able to raise only enough food to feed themselves and their families, with little left over to sell. The government is seeking to help the farmers through education, technical assistance, and better transportation.

Agriculture has wide variations, depending on the altitude and location. Corn, wheat, rice, potatoes, and cassava are the staple foods that Bolivians grow and eat. Farmers also grow such commercial crops as cacao, coca, coffee, and tropical fruits in the valleys. Sugarcane and soybeans are cultivated around Santa Cruz. Sugarcane was introduced to Bolivia at an early date. Much of it traditionally has gone into making rum. Soybeans have become Bolivia's leading agricultural export, after coca.

In the basins and valleys near Cochabamba, farmers grow wheat, corn, and barley. Along with vegetables and tropical fruits, these crops are sold to the cities in the Highlands. Valleys to the south are less densely populated and grow few crops for market. Near such large cities as Sucre and Tarija, however, farmers grow cereal grains and fruits. They also raise cattle and goats.

Livestock, Fishing, and Forestry

People have raised domesticated llamas and alpacas in the Andes since prehistoric times. Llamas are similar to camels in their usefulness in transportation. The fleece of both llamas and alpacas makes soft, warm clothing and especially fine coats, as well as rope.

Farmers raise almost 7 million head of cattle in many parts of Bolivia. In a few areas of the Lowlands, farmers breed cattle for beef on a large scale. Sheep graze freely on natural mountain pastures year-round. Other livestock include horses, mules, donkeys, pigs, rabbits, goats, guinea pigs (for food), chickens, turkeys, and ducks. Farmers also raise the chinchilla, a native rodent, for its luxurious fur and export its skin.

Fishing crews harvest Bolivia's many rivers. Aquaculture, or fish farming, produces tons of rainbow trout. Bolivians also hunt thousands of crocodiles, alligators, and caimans (a kind of crocodile) to export their skins for use in the fashion industry.

Although Bolivia has some of the best timber resources in the world, many forests are beyond the reach of modern transportation. The best forests of tropical trees—both evergreens and hardwoods—grow on the eastern slopes of the Andes and along the rivers of the Amazon basin. Rubber trees yielding high-quality rubber grow wild in the forests of Pando and El Beni in northern Bolivia. Brazil nuts grow wild on trees that often reach 100 feet (30 m) tall. In parts of southeastern Bolivia, forests of abundant hardwoods thrive. The woods include walnut and mahogany. Planters introduced

HEAVY DEBT

Since the 1952 revolution, Bolivia has received a lot of financial help from the governments of other countries, including the United States. It also has huge debts to privately owned foreign banks. The World Bank, a United Nations agency, has also loaned Bolivia massive amounts of money. While loans and aid have helped Bolivia develop, making payments on its huge foreign debt uses up much of the government's budget. Furthermore, some Bolivians resent that outside groups who loan Bolivia money sometimes want to control its economy too. In 2005 the Group of 8 (the G8—an organization of some of the world's most powerful countries) enacted a plan that forgave $2 billion of Bolivia's debt. The nation still owes almost $4 billion, however.

the eucalyptus tree from its native Australia in the nineteenth century. Eucalyptus groves near Cochabamba and Sucre supply fuel and wood for supports in mines.

Illegal Drug Trade

Coca is Bolivia's most valuable agricultural export. Bolivia is a leading world producer of coca leaves, which are used to make the drug cocaine. By the mid-1980s, experts estimate that the illegal drug trade in coca and refined cocaine brought Bolivia three times the profit of its leading mineral export. The profitable drug trade also spread corruption throughout society.

Smugglers transport most of the raw coca leaves to neighboring Latin American countries, where they are processed in makeshift labs. Most refined cocaine is exported to the United States. To discourage coca growing, the United States offered money to farmers who switch to other crops. Transportation for other crops, such as pineapples and bananas, is often lacking, however. These crops don't earn nearly as much as coca. Therefore, many Bolivian farmers never accepted the offer.

Plans to reduce coca production have met opposition from campesinos and sometimes have led to violence. President Morales legalized limited coca growing for traditional and medicinal uses, but many foreign governments strongly oppose this plan. Morales wants to market coca as a natural product, sold internationally in teas and even toothpaste, to stop its sale to the illegal drug trade.

The Future

Bolivia's democracy has triumphed over the country's history of coups and dictatorships. Bolivians still hotly debate how their economy is run, however. The nationalization of natural resources and industries has brought criticism from those who believe foreign investment is crucial. Others, however, point out that in the past, only a few Bolivians gained from private ownership of mines, industries, and land. If economic reforms do indeed bring a higher standard of living to the Bolivian people, the country faces a better future. Divisions between social classes still hamper Bolivians. But improved opportunities for Bolivia's indigenous people offer hope for a brighter future in the twenty-first century.

 Visit www.vgsbooks.com for links to websites with the latest information on Bolivia's economy, including news about mining and natural gas resources and issues affecting Bolivian businesses. Find out about the conversion rate for U.S. dollars into Bolivian bolivianos.

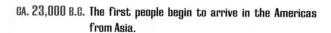

Timeline

CA. 23,000 B.C. The first people begin to arrive in the Americas from Asia.

CA. 8000 B.C. Early cultures develop in the Andes, including what will become Bolivia.

CA. 500 B.C. The Tiwanakan people begin to settle the shores of Lake Titicaca.

A.D. 900 The Tiwanakan Empire reaches its height during the coming century. A network of roads links its capital city of Tiwanaku to other communities. The city is home to about fifty thousand people.

CA. 1100 The Aymara civilization begins to arise in the Andes. Separate indigenous peoples of the eastern Lowlands live in small villages along rivers and in the rain forest.

CA. 1200 The Tiwanakan civilization disappears, possibly due to drought. The Inca Empire begins, ruled by a royal family from Cuzco in southern Peru.

CA. 1460 Inca armies invade and conquer Aymara lands. By 1500 the Inca have established a vast empire in western South America.

1532 Spaniard Francisco Pizarro leads fewer than two hundred soldiers in overthrowing the Inca royalty and beginning the conquest of the Inca Empire.

1538 Spanish conquerors establish the Viceroyalty of Peru and colonize Upper Peru—the land that will become Bolivia. They also found the city of Chuquisaca (Sucre) as its capital.

1572 Bolivia's peak period of silver production begins. It will last to 1630. During this era, forced labor in the mines at Potosí produce enormous amounts of silver. Colonists also use slaves to farm their estates.

1624 Colonists found the University of San Francisco Javier at present-day Sucre. It is one of the first universities in the Americas.

1781 Tupac Amarú II (José Gabriel Condorcanqui) and Tupac Katari (Julian Apaza) lead the Aymara in an independence movement for self-rule. About eighty thousand Aymara besiege La Paz, but the Spanish brutally put down the rebellion.

1809 The War of Independence begins on May 25, when the people of Chuquisaca (Sucre) revolt against Spain and establish their own government.

1825 Upper Peru wins independence on August 6. The new republic names itself Bolivia in honor of Simón Bolívar, who rules the country for six months and writes its constitution.

1879 The War of the Pacific breaks out among Peru, Chile, and Bolivia. By the end of the war, in 1883, Bolivia will have lost to Chile its mineral-rich lands along the Pacific coast and become landlocked.

1920   The government puts down an indigenous peoples' rebellion for justice.

1932   The Chaco War breaks out between Bolivia and Paraguay. About fifty thousand Bolivians will die in the fighting before the war ends in Bolivia's defeat in 1935.

1942   Forces of the military government kill hundreds of miners striking for better conditions in an event known as the Catavi Massacre.

1952   After years of military rule, the MNR-led victory in the Revolution of 1952 leads to democratic, civilian government, voting rights for all Bolivians, and state control of the mines.

1964   General René Barrientos Ortuño takes part in a military coup and rules as a dictator, ending civilian rule.

1967   The Bolivian army, with the help of the United States, captures and executes revolutionary Ernesto "Che" Guevara.

1979   Lidia Gueiler Tejada becomes Bolivia's first (and, as of the early 2000s, only) female president.

1982   Marking the return of civilian rule, Bolivians reelect Hernán Siles Zuazo. The decade sees world-record inflation, reaching 22,000 percent.

1994   Changes to the Bolivian constitution recognize Aymara and Quechua as official languages and lower the voting age to eighteen.

1997   President Hugo Banzer Suárez begins a "zero coca" plan and orders special police units to destroy coca crops. Juan Evo Morales Ayma, leader of the coca growers' union, defends small-scale farmers' rights to grow the crop.

2003   Riots leading to the deaths of more than ninety people force President Sánchez de Lozado to resign. Groups call for the nationalization of the country's natural resources.

2005   Juan Evo Morales Ayma, a Socialist, becomes Bolivia's first indigenous president, with 54 percent of the votes.

2006   President Morales's government nationalizes all of Bolivia's oil and gas resources. The nation has the second-largest natural gas reserves known in South America.

2007   Bolivians disapprove when the FIFA bans Bolivia from hosting international soccer matches due to its extreme altitude.

COUNTRY NAME Republic of Bolivia

AREA 425,000 square miles (1.1 million sq. km.)

MAIN LANDFORMS Andes Mountains; the altiplano; Sub-Andean yungas (valleys); lowland plains; Salar de Uyuni (salt flats)

HIGHEST POINT Nevado Sajama, 21,464 feet (6,542 m)

LOWEST POINT Paraguay River, 300 feet (90 m)

MAJOR RIVERS AND LAKES Beni, Desaguadero, Grande, Iténez, Mamoré, Paraguay, Pilcomayo, and San Miguel; Lake Titicaca, Lake Poopó

ANIMALS alpacas, anteaters, armadillos, capybaras, coatis, guanacos, jaguars, llamas, pumas, river dolphins, spectacled bears, swamp deer, tapirs, vicuñas, wildcats; alligators, boa constrictors, lizards, pit vipers, turtles; catfish, electric eels, piranhas, stingrays; condors, eagles, hummingbirds, macaws, parrots, rheas, toucans

CAPITAL CITIES La Paz (executive and legislative) and Sucre (judicial)

OTHER MAJOR CITIES Santa Cruz, Cochabamaba, Potosí

OFFICIAL LANGUAGES Spanish, Aymara, and Quechua

MONETARY UNIT Boliviano (BOB). 1 boliviano = 100 centavos.

CURRENCY

The boliviano replaced the peso as Bolivia's unit of currency in 1987. Coins come in values of 10, 20, and 50 centavos, and 1, 2, and 5 bolivianos. Banknotes, or paper money, come in denominations of 10, 20, 50, 100, and 200 bolivianos. The images on Bolivia's money show famous people, sites, and historic events. The 10 bolivianos note, for instance, depicts the artist Cecilio Guzman de Rojas. The "Heroinas de la Coronilla," or the Heroines of Coronilla, appear on the other side. These are the women who defended Cochabamba from Spanish forces during the War of Independence and are remembered on May 27—Mother's Day in Bolivia.

Bolivia adopted its current flag on November 30, 1851. It replaced the first flag of 1825 but kept its red and green colors for the top and bottom of its three horizontal bands. Red stands for strength and pride, and green stands for agriculture and growth. The flag's central yellow band represents the country's mineral wealth. The national bird, the Andean condor, sits atop the coat of arms in the center of the flag.

Bolivia adopted its national anthem in 1852. José Ignacio de Sanjinés, who wrote the words, signed both Bolivia's Declaration of Independence and its first constitution. Leopoldo Benedetto Vincenti, an Italian, wrote the music. Below is the song in Spanish (without the chorus) with an English translation.

"Canción Patriótica" (Patriotic Song)

Spanish	English Translation
Bolivianos el hado propicio	Bolivians, a favorable destiny,
coronó nuestros votos y anhelo	Has crowned our vows and
es ya libre, ya libre este suelo,	longings;
ya cesó su servil condición.	This land is free,
Al estruendo marcial que ayer	Your servile state has ended.
fuera	The martial turmoil of yesterday,
y al clamor de la guerra horroroso,	And the horrible clamor of war,
siguen hoy en contraste armo-nioso	Are followed today, in harmo-nious contrast,
dulces himnos de paz y de unión.	By sweet hymns of peace and unity.
Siguen hoy en contraste armo-nioso	Are followed today, in harmo-nious contrast,
dulces himnos de paz y de unión.	By sweet hymns of peace and unity.

 Find a link to what the melody of Bolivia's national anthem, "Canción Patriótica," sounds like at www.vgsbooks.com.

TUPAC AMARÚ II (1740–1781) Born in Tinta, Peru, José Gabriel Condorcanqui was a descendant of the last of the Inca rulers, Tupac Amarú, whom the Spanish executed in 1574. Though Condorcanqui was of indigenous heritage, he was wealthy and well educated in Spanish culture. He took the name Tupac Amarú II and began to plan a rebellion to return Bolivian lands to the native people. He gathered support from indigenous peoples of the Andes in his quest to restore the Inca monarchy. In 1780 he led his followers in an open revolt against Spanish rule. The Spanish defeated and executed Tupac Amarú II in 1781. He remains a hero to freedom-loving Bolivians.

JAIME ESCALANTE (b. 1930) Born in La Paz, Escalante became a math and physics teacher. He moved to the United States in 1964. There he taught in a drug- and crime-ridden high school in East Los Angeles, California. He became famous when he inspired a small group of his disadvantaged math students to study for and pass the AP (advanced placement) calculus test. This success was the subject of the popular 1988 movie *Stand and Deliver*. After winning many awards for his teaching, Escalante returned to Bolivia in 2001. He teaches part-time at a college in Cochabamba.

BERNARDO GUARACHI (b. 1953) A descendant of the Aymara people, Guarachi is a world-class mountain climber and guide. Born in Patacamaya—a village high in the Andes—he has spent most of his life above 16,666 feet (5,000 m). His family raised sheep and llamas. Guarachi has climbed Mount Illimani, one of the highest peaks in South America, more than 170 times. In 1985 Eastern Airlines hired him to find an airplane that crashed into Illimani on New Year's Day. In 1998 Guarachi became the first Bolivian and first indigenous American to reach the summit of Mount Everest, the highest peak in the world.

LIDIA GUEILER TEJADA (b. 1921) Gueiler was the first woman president of Bolivia, serving from 1979–1980. Born in Cochabamba, Gueiler became an accountant. After the 1952 revolution, she was a member of Congress from 1956 to 1964. When the revolution failed in 1964, she left the country. After she returned to Bolivia in 1979, she was elected to be the leader of the lower house of Congress. Turmoil followed the 1979 presidential elections. Military, political, and labor union leaders chose Gueiler to lead the nation until new elections could be held in 1980. She was the second female head of state in Latin America (Isabel Peron of Argentina was the first). Shortly before the elections, however, General Luis García Meza, led the bloody 169th coup in Bolivia's history and overthrew the government. Gueiler moved to France until 1982, when civilian rule was restored. She served Bolivia as ambassador to other countries until she retired in the mid-1990s. Gueiler supports the presidency of Evo Morales.

JAIME LAREDO (b. 1941) Laredo is an internationally famous violinist. Born in Cochabamba, he began playing the violin when he was five and began performing when he was eight. Laredo moved to the United States to study music. He plays and conducts music around the world, including performing at the U.S. White House. Laredo has recorded more than forty albums. His recording of music by classical composer Brahms won a Grammy Award in 1991. Laredo also performs the work of modern composers. Bolivia named a stadium in La Paz after Laredo and honored him in a set of postage stamps.

JUAN EVO MORALES AYMA (b. 1959) Bolivia's president since January 2006, Morales was born in Isallavi, near Lake Poopó. He is the first fully indigenous president of Bolivia. He grew up in a poor Aymara family. Only four of the family's seven children survived. Morales recalls playing soccer with his dog, using a rag ball, while he herded llamas when he was a boy. He ran for president on a promise to take government control of Bolivia's natural resources and to empower Bolivia's oppressed people. True to his pledge, he soon began to nationalize the country's natural gas and oil industries. He also cut his own salary in half so the government could hire more teachers. Morales works closely with President Hugo Chavez of Venezuela. Both presidents are eager to be free of U.S. influence and aid. Morales also faces many challenges as he plans to legalize coca growing while ending the illegal cocaine trade.

MARINA NÚÑEZ DEL PRADO (1910–1995) Núñez del Prado studied art at the Fine Arts Academy in her hometown of La Paz. She went on to teach sculpture at the school. She is known as one of Latin America's most famous sculptors. The rolling curves of her early works reflect her love of music and dance. Indian themes inspired her, and her pieces also capture pumas, bulls, the majestic condor, and other Andean animals. Using tropical woods, bronze, marble, and other materials, Núñez del Prado expressed her concern for social issues in works such as *Miners in Revolt* (1946). Her art often features the human body, especially female figures, as seen in the white onyx sculpture *White Venus* (1960) and the bronze *Andean Women in Flight* (1988).

ADELA ZAMUDIO (1854–1928) Considered one of Bolivia's best poets, Zamudio was born and spent her life in Cochabamba. She published her first poem, "Two Roses," when she was fifteen, but a book of her poetry did not appear for another twenty years. Zamudio was also a painter, short-story writer, and a teacher. Her poetry was romantic, but her politics were radical for the times. In her poem "To Be Born a Man," Zamudio condemned the oppression of women. She wrote many articles calling for democratic reforms and women's rights, such as legalizing divorce. (Divorce laws would not pass in Bolivia until 1932.) The poet sometimes used the pseudonym Soledad, which means "loneliness" in Spanish.

THE CHE GUEVARA TRAIL The Bolivian government opened this 510-mile (820 km) trail in 1997—the thirtieth anniversary of the revolutionary's death. Hikers can trace the last steps of Che and his small band as they tried to escape from the Bolivian army. The trail winds through the region around La Higuera in the eastern Lowlands.

COCHABAMBA Bolivia's "boom city" is growing rapidly. Set in a fertile valley, Cochabamba's perfect climate lends it the nickname City of Eternal Spring. Colonial houses and churches—including the cathedral, dating to 1571—preserve the historical flavor in the old center of town. Lively markets and flowering trees in parks and plazas add color. Cochabamba's wide streets offer restaurants and a lively nightlife.

ISLA DEL SOL (ISLAND OF THE SUN) Visitors can take a boat trip on Lake Titicaca to this large island in the lake. It is the legendary birthplace of the Incas, and Inca and pre-Inca ruins cover the island. The villages on the island seem to exist in the long-ago past. In Yumani, the island's main port, a long stairway leads to a fountain from which flow three streams. These streams symbolize the ancient three-part Inca law: don't steal, lie, or be lazy.

NOEL KEMPFF MERCADO NATIONAL PARK This 3.8-million-acre (1.5 million hectares) park in remote northeastern Bolivia is one of the best-preserved parks in the vast Amazon basin. In 2000 the United Nations placed the park on the World Heritage list. Its many habitats boast an estimated 4,000 kinds of plants and more than 620 bird species. including 20 kinds of parrots. Hikers may spot tapirs, howler monkeys, giant otters, or some of the park's more than 130 kinds of mammals. Many threatened species, such as the pink river dolphin, survive in the park.

ORURO Folk dancing and partying fill the streets of Oruro for the entire week of Carnaval, right before Lent. Colorful costumes, energizing music, and water fights mark this most famous of Latin American fiestas. The city was founded in 1601 in southwestern Bolivia.

POTOSÍ About 50 miles (80 km) southwest of Sucre, this mining city is one of Bolivia's six UNESCO World Heritage Sites. At its peak in the 1600s, Potosí was the largest city in the Americas, due to its enormous deposits of silver. The city's elevation of 13,400 feet (4,000 m) makes it the highest city of its size in the world.

TIWANAKU The temples and monuments of this ancient Tiwanakan city formed the spiritual and political center of one of the world's greatest civilizations. A small museum on the site helps visitors understand this culture, which flourished more than one thousand years ago. The Gate of the Sun (Puerta del Sol) stands at the city's northwest corner. Visitors can also see residential homes and the artists' quarters. The city covers 1,482 acres (600 hectares).

Aymara: a person of Bolivia's indigenous Aymara ethnic group or one of Bolivia's official languages. The Aymara live in the Andes and are descendants of the Tiwanakan civilization.

campesino: a rural dweller. In Bolivia campesinos are usually small-scale, poor farmers of indigenous heritage.

capitalism: an economic system of private ownership

cholo: a mestizo, or person of mixed Indian and European ancestry. Usually of the middle classes, Bolivian cholos speak Spanish and follow Western ways.

Communism: a political and economic theory that proposes no private ownership. Its goal is to create equality. In a wholly Communist society, all goods would be owned in common.

coup: a sudden, often violent, overthrow of a government. *Coup* means "blow" in French.

dictator: a leader who rules with complete control, often through the use of harsh methods

encomienda: a Spanish colonial system that gave Spanish settlers land and rights to the labor of indigenous people. The colonists were supposed to protect and educate the Indians in the Christian religion. Many colonists instead exploited them as slaves.

gross domestic product (GDP): the value of the goods and services produced by a country over a period of time, usually one year

junta: a group that controls a government, especially one that has violently taken power

land reform: measures a government takes to redistribute farmland more equitably among its people

Latin America: Mexico, Central America, South America, and the islands of the West Indies. Latin America includes thirty-three independent countries, including Bolivia, and thirteen other political units.

literacy: the ability to read and write

Quechua: a member of Bolivia's largest indigenous ethnic group, or the language of the Incas and one of Bolivia's official languages

rain forest: dense woodland that receives more than 100 inches (250 cm) of rainfall per year

Socialism: a variety of social systems in which the government controls and manages some part of the production and distribution of goods

Selected Bibliography

BBC News. 2007.
http://www.bbc.co.uk **(April 2007).**
The World Edition of the BBC (British Broadcasting Company) News is updated throughout the day, every day. The BBC is a source for comprehensive news coverage about Bolivia. It also provides a country profile at http://news.bbc.co.uk/1/hi/world/ americas/country_profiles/1210487.stm.

Buckman, Robert T. *Latin America 2006*. Harpers Ferry, WV: Stryker-Post Publications, 2006.
Part of the annual World Today series, this publication includes a long article on Bolivia. It presents an overview of the country's history, government, culture, and economy.

Central Intelligence Agency (CIA). "Bolivia." *The World Factbook*. 2007.
http://www.cia.gov/cia/publications/factbook/geos/bl.html **(March 2007).**
This CIA website provides facts and figures on Bolivia's geography, people, government, economy, communications, transportation, military, and more.

Energy Information Administration. *Country Analysis Brief: Bolivia*. October 2006.
http://www.eia.doe.gov/emeu/cabs/Bolivia/Background.html **(March 2007).**
This site is one of the most complete sources of energy statistics on the Internet. It offers information about energy production and use in Bolivia and other countries of the world. The site also includes Web links and a kids' section about energy.

Klein, Herbert S. *A Concise History of Bolivia*. Cambridge: University of Cambridge Press, 2003.
Klein, a professor of Latin American history, surveys Bolivia's economic, social, cultural, and political growth. This book explores pre-Columbian civilizations, the colonial society, the 1952 revolution, and the challenges of creating a democratic society after 1982 into the early twenty-first century.

Library of Congress. Federal Research Division. *A Country Study: Bolivia*. 1989/2006. http://lcweb2.loc.gov/frd/cs/bolivia/html **(March 2007).**
The site accesses the book-length 1989 country study and also provides a link to the updated *Country Profile: Bolivia*, January 2006. The U.S. Federal Research Division's studies cover the main historical, social, economic, political, and national security aspects of Bolivia. Sources of information include scholarly publications, official reports and documents of government and international organizations, and foreign and domestic newspapers and periodicals.

Lopez Levy, Marcela. *Bolivia*. Oxford, UK: Oxfam GB, 2001.
Oxfam is an international aid organization. Its Country Profiles series is designed to look at international social, economic, and environmental issues and especially to focus on the real lives of ordinary people. This book from the series examines the indigenous majority of Bolivia and their claims to be heard and to participate in the nation's political process.

Morales, Waltraud Q. *A Brief History of Bolivia*. New York: Facts on File, 2003.

This book presents an overview of Bolivia's history from its ancient civilizations to the early twenty-first century. It also covers Bolivia's ethnic makeup, the challenges the nation's extreme landscapes and climate present, and the state of human rights and issues of illegal drugs. Extras include maps, photographs, a chronology, and a complete bibliography.

Murphy, Alan. *Bolivia Handbook*. Bath, UK: Footprint Handbooks, 1997.

A comprehensive travel guidebook, this title also offers fascinating information about Bolivia, such as coca use as a way of life and Butch Cassidy and the Sundance Kid's deaths in San Vicente, Bolivia. More up-to-date travel information about Bolivia may be found in Ben Box's *Footprint South American Handbook, 2007*, by the same publisher.

Nystrom, Andrew Dean, and Morgan Konn. *Bolivia*. Melbourne: Lonely Planet Publications, 2004.

This travel guidebook offers advice on how to wind through mountain passes and jungle Lowlands or experience Bolivia's markets and festivals. It also provides good, brief overviews of the country's history, environment, and culture.

Population Reference Bureau. 2006. http://www.prb.org (March 2007).

PRB provides annual, in-depth demographics on Bolivia's population. It includes birthrates and death rates, infant mortality rates, and other statistics relating to health, environment, education, employment, family planning, and more. Special articles cover environmental and health issues.

***South America, Central America and the Caribbean 2007*. London: Routledge, 2007.**

This is a volume in the Europa Regional Surveys of the World series. The long section on Bolivia in this annual publication covers the country's recent history, geography, and culture. It also provides a detailed look at the economy, politics, and government of the nation. Statistics and sources are included too.

U.S. Department of State, Bureau of Western Hemisphere Affairs. *Background Note: Bolivia*. March 2007.

http://www.state.gov/r/pa/ei/bgn/35751.htm (April 2007).

The background notes of the U.S. State Department supplies a profile of Bolivia's people, history, government, political conditions, and economy. The State Department also provides travel information for Americans going abroad.

Augustin, Byron. *Bolivia.* **Danbury, CT: Children's Press, 2001.**
Part of the Enchantment of the World series for younger readers, this volume offers colorful photos, maps, and charts. Chapters describe the history, geography, economy, language, and culture of Bolivia.

Bolivia Web
http://www.boliviaweb.com
This site provides links to Bolivian newspapers and more than five hundred blogs about the country. It also offers information on Bolivia's culture, politics, land, travel, and more.

Cruxton, J. Bradley. *Discovering the Amazon Rainforest.* **Don Mills, ON: Oxford University Press Canada, 1998.**
This book takes the younger reader into the tropical rain forest along the Amazon River. It offers a look at plants, animals, and human ways of life in the forest. Environmental issues are also examined.

Ghinsberg, Yossi. *Jungle: A Harrowing True Story of Survival.* **Austin, TX: Boomerang New Media, 2006.**
The rain forest of Bolivia comes alive in this book about the author's struggle for survival in the wild. Ghinsberg headed into what he thought would be a dream adventure with three backpackers he met in La Paz, Bolivia. Soon the group split up, and Ghinsberg found himself lost and alone. His tale of making his way back to civilization makes gripping reading.

Guevara, Ernesto Che. *The Bolivian Diary.* **New York: Ocean Press, 2006.**
This is the last diary of famous revolutionary Che Guevara, written during his attempts to start a revolution in Bolivia. The entries begin in November 1966 and record Guevara's travels with a small force through rugged, rainy terrain. Their life included eating wild animals such as tapirs. The last entry is October 7, 1967, the night before the Bolivian army captured Guevara. The same directors who created a film version in 2004 of Guevara's youthful journal *The Motorcycle Diaries* are making a film based on this diary.

Gumucio Dagron, Alfonso. *Making Waves: Stories of Participatory Communication for Social Change.* **The Rockefeller Foundation.**
http://www.comminit.com/strategicthinking/pdsmakingwaves/sld-2593.html.
The English-language version of *Making Waves* by Bolivian author Gumucio Dagron is out of print. The entire report is available at this website. Especially interesting is the chapter about the role of radio in the lives of Chilean miners.

Havelin, Kate. *Che Guevara.* **Minneapolis: Twenty-First Century Books, 2007.**
This biography follows Che Guevara's life, from his impoverished childhood to his career as a South American revolutionary. Unwelcome in Argentina, his homeland, and frustrated with his efforts to make change in Africa, he arrived in Bolivia in 1966 with hopes of igniting a Communist revolution there. He and his small band of fighters made history during their year in Bolivia.

Further Reading and Websites

Hermes, Jules. *The Children of Bolivia.* **Minneapolis: Lerner Publications Company, 1996.**
Author and photographer Hermes provides an intriguing glimpse of everyday life in Bolivia through the lives of some of the country's children. Some, like Maria, live much as their ancestors did, while others live modern urban lifestyles, complete with fast-food restaurants.

Knutson, Barbara. *Love and Roast Chicken: A Trickster Tale from the Andes Mountains.* **Minneapolis: Carolrhoda Books, 2004.**
This folktale from Peru and Bolivia is typical of the trickster tales in which a smaller, weaker animal uses its smarts to outwit a more powerful enemy. In this case, Cuy, a guinea pig, cleverly outwits a hungry fox and a powerful farmer. This book for younger readers is illustrated with woodblock and water-color prints. It includes a glossary and pronunciation guides for the text's Spanish and Quechua words.

Maynard, Charles W. *The Andes.* **New York: Rosen Publishing, 2004.**
This book is part of the Great Mountain Ranges of the World series for younger readers. Well illustrated, it looks at the geology and the people, plants, and animals of the Andes.

Olivera, Oscar. *¡Cochabamba! Water War in Bolivia.* **Cambridge, MA: South End Press, 2004.**
Oscar Olivera works as a machinist in Cochabamba. In 2000 he helped form a grassroots movement that led thousands of people to protest the sale of the local water company to a U.S.-based company. *¡Cochabamba!* is his story of how these water activists regained control of their water supply.

Parnell, Helga. *Cooking the South American Way.* **Minneapolis: Lerner Publications Company, 2003.**
The many cultures of South America feature a variety of dishes. Focusing on recipes from countries including Bolivia, Brazil, and Chile, this cookbook offers a sampling of tastes from across the continent. It also gives a brief overview of the land and people.

vgsbooks.com
http://www.vgsbooks.com
Visit vgsbooks.com, the home page of the Visual Geography Series®, which is updated regularly. You can get linked to all sorts of useful online information, including geographical, historical, demographic, cultural, and economic websites. The vgsbooks.com site is a great resource for late-breaking news and statistics.

Young-Sánchez, Margaret. *Tiwanaku: Ancestors of the Inca.* **Denver: Denver Art Museum, 2004.**
The Denver Art Museum published this beautifully illustrated book to accompany an exhibition of the same name. It depicts in full-color photographs of artifacts of the ancient Tiwanakan civilization of Bolivia. Essays help the reader understand this little-known culture.

Captions for photos appearing on cover and chapter openers:

Cover: Cones of harvested salt await transport from the Salar de Uyuni salt flats to processing facilities, where the salt will be iodized and exported.

pp. 4–5 Terraced fields and Inca ruins cover the steep hills of Isla del Sol (Island of the Sun) in Lake Titicaca.

pp. 8–9 Mount Illimani rises above the town of Laja on the altiplano. Laja was the first capital of Bolivia until the Spanish chose to relocate the government center to La Paz in 1898.

pp. 20–21 The Gate of the Sun stands in the ruins of Tiwanaku. Ancient artists carved this massive portal from a single block of stone. Its carvings feature typical Tiwanakan motifs, including puma faces, condors, and a snake with a human face.

pp. 38–39 Three Aymara women pose with their llamas on the shores of Lake Titicaca.

pp. 46–47 Dancers dressed as devils and gods parade through the streets of Oruro during the La Diablada (Devil Dances) festival.

pp. 58–59 Farmworkers in Los Yungas harvest coca leaves for traditional use as painkillers and stimulants. Bolivian farmers defend their right to grow and sell coca despite pressure from countries that object to the export of coca to manufacturers of the illegal drug cocaine.

Photo Acknowledgments

The images in this book are used with the permission of: © Mary Jelliffe/Art Directors, pp. 4–5, 8–9; © XNR Productions, pp. 6, 10; © Hubertus Kanus/SuperStock, p. 11; © age fotostock/SuperStock, pp. 13, 16 (left), 20–21, 58–59, 60; © Norman Price/Art Directors, p. 14; © Ken Lucas/Visuals Unlimited, p. 16 (right); © James May/SuperStock, pp. 18–19; © AAAC/Topham/The Image Works, p. 23; The Granger Collection, New York, p. 25; Library of Congress, p. 26 (LC-US262-51627); © Kurt Severin/Stringer/Hulton Archive/Getty Images, p. 29; © Keystone/Hulton Archive/Getty Images, p. 31; AP Photo, p. 32; © Gonzalo Espinoza/AFP/Getty Images, p. 34; © Bru Garcia/AFP/Getty Images, p. 36; © Angelo Cavalli/SuperStock, pp. 38–39; © Zack Seckler/Getty Images, p. 41; © SuperStock, Inc./SuperStock, p. 42; © Dermot Tatlow/Panos Pictures, p. 43; © Mireille Vautier/Alamy, pp. 44–45; © Christopher Pillitz/Reportage/Getty Images, pp. 46-47; © Henri Szwarc/Bongarts/Getty Images, p. 49; © Melanie Stetson Freeman/Christian Science Monitor/Getty Images, pp. 51, 55; © Ernest Manewal/SuperStock, p. 52; © Aizar Raldes/AFP/Getty Images, p. 53; © Frans Lemmens/The Image Bank/Getty Images, p. 54; © Tibor Bognar/Art Directors, p. 56; © Prisma/SuperStock, p. 62; Audrius Tomonis—www.banknotes.com, p. 68; © Laura Westlund/Independent Picture Service, p. 69.

Cover photo: © Tui De Roy/Minden Pictures/Getty Images. Back cover: NASA.